leaders

who will last

10TH ANNIVERSARY EDITION

Leaders who will last: 10th anniversary edition
Copyright © Tim Hawkins/The Good Book Company 2010

The Good Book Company
Elm House, 37 Elm Road, New Malden, Surrey KT3 3HB, UK
Telephone: 0333 123 0880 International: +44 (0) 208 942 0880
email: admin@thegoodbook.co.uk

Websites:
UK: www.thegoodbook.co.uk
N America: www.thegoodbook.com
Australia: www.thegoodbook.com.au
New Zealand: www.thegoodbook.co.nz

Hawkins Ministry Resources
PO Box 7569, Baulkham Hills Business Centre, NSW, 2153
Fax: (+61 2) 9629 6569
E-mail: info@hawkinsministry.com
Website: www.hawkinsministry.com

Unless otherwise indicated, Scripture verses taken from the HOLY
BIBLE, NEW INTERNATIONAL VERSION. Copyright ©1973, 1978, 1984
International Bible Society. Used by permission of Zondervan Bible
Publishers.

All rights reserved. No part of this publication may be reproduced,
stored in a retrieval system, or transmitted on any form or by any means
– electronic, mechanical, photocopy, recording, or any other – except for
brief quotations in printed reviews, without the prior permission of the
publisher.

ISBN: 9781907377440

Cover design by Steve Devane
Printed in the UK

Preface to this 10th anniversary edition

Leadership is so important. Without strong leadership, nations do not prosper; companies do not succeed; sporting teams do not triumph; individuals do not achieve their potential. Without effective leadership there is no valuing of the past, there is no way forward through the present, and there is no hope for the future.

When Jesus came to earth to bring the most effective transformation that could ever be accomplished, he spent most of his three years of public ministry developing his leadership team. His twelve. The ones he would commission to spread his life-changing message to every nation of this planet.

Local church youth ministry suffers when leadership is weak. There is no spiritual progress when youth leaders are not developed to the same high level as leadership in other parts of the church. In my thirty-plus years of being involved in youth ministry in local churches the biggest obstacle, in human terms, has been a failure in leadership.

The reason for this book? Simply to take the biblical pictures of leadership and apply them to youth leaders in the twenty-first century. The reason for a tenth anniversary edition? God is still teaching me many things, and this comprehensive revision reflects my journey for the ten years since it was first published.

I pray that this book will take you back to biblical truths which will inspire you to keep becoming the leader that God has designed you to be.

John Warren—Guest contributor

I want to acknowledge the major contribution by John Warren to the writing of this book. John served with me as a faithful part-time staff member in the mid nineties, and he has had a profound effect on my life. I believe that John, and his fantastic wife Catherine, will have a significant ministry in years to come.

When I came to the section on "Growing your Character", I could think of no better material than what John had written on these topics some years ago. With John's kind permission, I have edited and reproduced much of his original work. The bulk of Chapters 8, 9 10 and 11 has been contributed by John.

Thanks heaps...

To Jesus Christ. Without you, not only would there be no book, but I would have no life. You have taken me to the Father, and filled me with your Spirit. Without you, I can do nothing.

To my wife, Karen. Without you, I could not do this ministry. I deeply appreciate the way you put up with me as I wrote each page. I love you!

To my children Carly and Joshua. "Out there" youth ministry means nothing compared with the joy of seeing you into Christian adulthood.

To Wayne Alcorn. You first opened my eyes to the possibility of being a "generation changer".

To the students and leaders at "Crossfire" in sunny downtown Castle Hill. Thank you for allowing me to take you on the exciting journey of having your life turned around by Jesus.

I have taken great care to give due credit to those who have impacted my life and ministry. It is possible that I have inadvertently included material which has not been properly acknowledged. If this has happened, please contact the publisher so that this can be rectified in future editions.

Contents

Section 4. Appendices

SECTION 1

Grow your leadership vision

Chapter 1
You are called by God

1. Am I the right person for this job?

"Would you like to help lead our youth group?"

The words sounded innocent enough. I mean, what could be that hard about being a youth leader? And I guess I felt kind of important. "Who, me?"

It sounded good! It would look good on my resumé. It would boost my self esteem. I was impressed that I had been asked. I was sure my friends would be impressed. Probably even God would be impressed!

"What does it involve?"

"Not much—just help lead a Bible-study group. You know, help plan it, help teach it, take responsibility for it."

Sounded good to me. Why not? What did I have to lose?

My first Bible-study group went okay. I had read the notes—I knew what to teach. The kids were great. The atmosphere was fun. Kids **liked** me. I liked them. This was cool. No one had ever paid me much attention before. These kids were actually looking up to me. Listening to me (occasionally!). Looking to me for answers. Believing what I taught them. Seeking my guidance. Starting to live their lives the way I told them...

Hang on... *"Starting to live their life the way I told them"?* This was scary stuff! What if I got it wrong? What if they took my advice and ended up in a heap of trouble? **These students were depending on me.** What if I let them down?

I remember the first time I went away on a camp as a youth leader. I was a cabin leader. I had six junior-high boys to take care of. They were full of energy and boundless enthusiasm. They were fun; they were foolish; they were fierce; they were high-octane flatulence machines... but I loved them. And here's the scary bit—**I** was in charge of them. Caring for them, listening to them, teaching them, keeping them from wreaking untold havoc upon the world that could have easily resulted in grievous personal bodily harm and the mother-of-all-lawsuits.

I was responsible for them. On the first night, I was having trouble sleeping. Eventually the room was deathly quiet, and I was aware that I was probably the only one awake. So I got up for a little while, and stood in the middle of our cabin. In the faint moonlight I walked around and glanced at each person. Each one was sound asleep. Each one was at rest. Whatever had gone on in their day, it was all behind them. They trusted me to look after them. In their sleep they were relying on me—depending on me—trusting me.

Then it hit me. **They were trusting their safety and their future into my hands.** I was in a position of awesome trust, and awesome responsibility. Man—did I feel inadequate! Why me? What made me the right person for this job? How could I lead these young men? I was still sorting out my own life! I was young. I hadn't had that much training. I'd only been a Christian for a short time myself. Surely God had someone better than me for this awesome responsibility!

How could one inadequate person possibly make a difference in the lives of any of these fragile teenagers?

2. God chooses the strangest people

Throughout history, we see that God often chooses the strangest people to achieve what he wants. When he wants to influence a nation—when he wants to lead his people—when he wants to call crowds to turn back and follow him—he often calls an individual person to lead them. God doesn't have to do it this way—but he chooses to involve us in his mighty plans. The pages of Scripture are a record of how God achieves mighty miracles with huge numbers of people—and he often accomplishes this by choosing just one person to lead them.

Some quick examples:

a) Abram (you probably know him as "Abraham"!)

Even before God had ever formed his Old Testament nation of Israel, he called on one man—Abram—to lead the whole shebang. Before they had any land—before they had any people—before anything at all had happened to gather God's people together so they could worship him as one nation—God called on Abram to be their leader.

> *The LORD had said to Abram, "Leave your country, your people and your father's household and go to the land I will show you.* **Genesis 12:1**

How about that for an invitation to a leadership position? Did you note what God asked Abram to do?

   i.   *Leave his country* (and he didn't give him an airline ticket).

    ii.   *Leave his own culture* (he would be ministering to people who were "different").

    iii.   *Leave his own family* (cutting him off from every support he had).

    iv.   *Go to a land "that I will show you"* (he had no idea where God would lead him).

    *By faith Abraham, when called to go to a place he would later receive as his inheritance, obeyed and went, **even though he did not know where he was going.***   **Hebrews 11:8**

Through that one man, Abraham, God established his own people—his own nation—a world power that would influence other nations to turn to God—and set the stage for the mighty works he would do throughout eternity.

To achieve all that, God called one man to lead his people. That one man—Abraham.

b) Moses
God's people were in slavery in Egypt. God had not forgotten the promises he had made to Abraham. He planned to rescue his people from the slavery of Egypt, overpower the evil Pharaoh who held them in shackles, and lead them out as conquerors toward the new land that he would give them.

To achieve all this, God raised up one man—one leader—Moses.

Firstly, God got Moses' attention with a burning bush—then he declared his great plan to rescue his people out of slavery—and then there's the crunch point for Moses:

*So now, go. I am sending **you** to Pharaoh to bring my people the Israelites out of Egypt.*   ***Exodus 3:10***

"Who, me?"

I think that's what I would have said!

"I mean, it's a nice plan to rescue your people—free us from slavery—overpower the evil Pharaoh—and lead us out to this land you promised to us, but you want me to lead all this? You've got to be joking!"

That's what Moses said too! He came up with all sorts of excuses: all sorts of reasons why he was the wrong man and all sorts of plausible arguments as to why he was absolutely the wrong person. But God had something mighty planned—God had the destiny of a whole nation that he wanted to change. So he raised up one man—Moses—to be the leader that he wanted.

c) David

By the time we get to the story of David, we see that God had now established his Old Testament nation of Israel. He was going to appoint a new leader—a new king to rule over his people. Who would he choose?

God had sent Samuel—his prophet—to go and anoint the new king. He had told him that one of Jesse's sons would be the new leader of his people. You can imagine the fuss at Jesse's house as all his sons lined up to impress the prophet who was about to arrive. They were on their best behaviour. Their hair was done and their shoes were shined. They had their "power suits" on. Mobile phones turned to "vibrate only". They only had one shot to make a good first impression. Who would win the job to be this new leader that God was going to choose?

Samuel walked through this parade of leadership wannabes. Some were tall, some were commanding, some were real leadership material. Jesse was no doubt anxious to see one of his boys become the new head honcho of everything God was doing.

> *Jesse made seven of his sons pass before Samuel, but Samuel said to him, "The LORD has not chosen these." So he asked Jesse, "Are these all the sons you have?" "There is still the youngest," Jesse answered, "but he is tending the sheep." Samuel said, "Send for him; we will not sit down until he arrives."*
> **1 Samuel 16:10-11**

God had one person in mind to lead his people. And it wasn't one of the executive parade that Jesse had lined up to impress the prophet. There was one more son—the kid brother, David. Not even old enough to be invited to the interview. Left to do all the work of tending the sheep while the big brothers showed off their talent. Not the person that any of us would have chosen.

And yet God chose the "little boy"—the runt of the family—to become the greatest king over all of Israel. Through King David, God's people grew in faithfulness and prosperity. It was David who was given the promises by God that Jesus himself would come from his family line.

God wanted a leader for his people. So he chose one person to be the leader who would accomplish what he had planned.

d) Paul

I really don't know what God was doing when he chose Paul to be his leader. I mean, look at his credentials! He opposed the name of Jesus. He persecuted Jesus' followers. He gave his permission for Christians to be killed. He was a man who had devoted his life to opposing everything that Jesus stood for.

And yet this was the very man whom God chose to influence the world in a way that no other had. It was Paul who took the message of Jesus to all the other nations of the planet. It was Paul who stepped into dangerous territory because God wanted his message to be for "all the nations"—and not just for his Old Testament people of Israel. God had a worldwide message—and he wanted it proclaimed "to the ends of the earth" (even to Australia and New Zealand!) It was Paul who wrote a great slab of our New Testament. Probably more people have been influenced through his ministry than practically anybody else.

God had a worldwide ministry to accomplish. So he chose this one man—Paul—to be his leader, and to accomplish great things.

3. But why me?

Who knows why God has chosen you to be a leader in his ministry? Who knows what great things he has planned for you? Who can count the number of people who will be influenced because of your faithfulness? Which nations of this planet will be changed for ever by the people you nurture and disciple? Who will be the one person who needs the tender touch of Jesus in their life—where God will use you to bring his word of comfort and healing?

If you look at it on paper, it was a ridiculous move for God to choose me to be a leader at all. I was a self-righteous moralist. I was full of my own accomplishments. I looked down on other people and their failures, and I had no time for flawed earthlings and their irritating habits. I lived in a self-contained world and viewed most folk as interruptions to my life's ambitions. I was **nothing like** the person who could be used by God to influence the lives of others! *(If you would like independent witnesses of where God has taken me from, then talk to my wife… or my sister… they knew me then!!)*

And yet God took me by the hand—and worked on me from the inside—and he changed my spirit and my character so that I could be used by him. I do not know why God has done that. If I were God, I would have given up on me ages ago!

If God is calling you to be a leader, I want to assure you that he has a purpose and a plan in mind. It is no accident. Maybe you got into leadership "because the pastor asked you to". Maybe "there was no one else". Perhaps in a moment of weakness you offered to help out for a week, and found that you were stuck with a job for life. But God is not a God of accidents and emergencies. He is a God of plan and purpose. You might not know **how** God will use you for his glory as you lead others, but I want to assure you that he **will** use you.

4. Welcome to the ranks of the foolish

God's plan is not to produce a team of super-leaders who will change the world with their natural charm and invincible powers. Rather, he chooses his faithful servants so that he can work powerfully through them.

> *But God chose the foolish things of the world to shame the wise; God chose the weak things of the world to shame the strong. He chose the lowly things of this world and the despised things—and the things*

*that are not—to nullify the things that are, so that no
one may boast before him.*   ***1 Corinthians 1:27-29***

God will use you—with whatever strengths and weaknesses
you have—so that he will accomplish his mighty things in
this world. The end result of this is not meant to be that
everyone will think, *"You're a great leader"*, but that people
will fall on their knees and say, *"God is a great God"*.

What a privilege! I get to be a fragile, imperfect creature, so
that others will see the immeasurable value of God's gospel
at work in my life. Cool!

Welcome to the world of Christian youth leadership.
Welcome to the ranks of the foolish. Let's journey together
so that we can learn how to be the leaders that God wants
us to be.

Leaders who will last.

Read on!

Chapter 2
You are a generation-changer

1. The problems of youth leadership

It had been a hard weekend. It was our annual youth-group weekend camp. About 30 high-schoolers in a remote location. Assorted leaders. A few weary cooks. A weekend dominated by raging hormones and punctuated with plentiful bodily functions. I was running the whole shebang. Presenting the Bible talks. Trying to keep everyone happy (including the somewhat crusty campsite manager). Making sure the whole weekend didn't descend into chaos.

The students had been restless. Well, that was probably putting it politely. They had been disruptive. Un-co-operative. Unresponsive. Friday night had stretched into the wee hours of Saturday morning, and by Saturday night, I was very tired. Eventually everyone had settled. They were in their beds. Asleep—or at least pretending to be. The midnight raids had stopped—the endless jokes accompanied by raucous laughter had dulled to mild snickers—and in the half-light of the dead of night I reflected on this scary and difficult world that we call "youth ministry".

I was ready to give up. I had been a faithful youth pastor for four years. But I felt I was losing my touch. I was a different generation from these teenagers. Too old. Out of touch. I was 28 years old. Maybe God was calling me to something else? *"Please, God, call me to something else! Anything!"*

But God wasn't ready for me to slip away quietly into a lower-stress job (such as an air-traffic controller!). He wasn't quite prepared for me to get out my blanket and sit in my rocking chair and claim: *"I'm too old to do youth ministry"*. It wasn't that the gap between me and the teenagers was too big. I discovered that the gap between me and **God** was too big! My vision was way too small. I saw myself as an insignificant youth pastor having a small effect on a handful of teenagers. I saw myself as a leader who organised programmes and ran the youth group. I saw myself as someone who simply tried to get uninterested teenagers to understand the Bible, and I felt terribly discouraged whenever I felt I had failed.

2. The vision of youth leadership

If you are a youth leader, you are not in some small-time ministry that doesn't really matter. You are not baby-sitting teenagers until a "real" minister can do some "real" work with them when they grow to be "real" people. **You have been called by God into one of the most significant ministries on the planet!** You have been thrust by God into working with people at their most significant time of change. You have the privilege of getting alongside adolescents at the moment when they are making decisions that will alter the direction of their entire life. You get to challenge and equip a young army of workers who have a lifetime ahead of them to infect this planet with the message of Jesus and to bring about a generational change which you and I can only dream about.

You are not some small-time youth leader running unimportant, peripheral programmes. You have been called by God to be a generation-changer!

David captures this thought powerfully in Psalm 71:

Even when I am old and grey, do not forsake me, O
God, till I declare your power to the next generation,
your might to all who are to come.   **Psalm 71:18**

Imagine the privilege of: *"declaring God's power to the*
next generation"! Wow! We get to pass on to a whole new
generation the amazing love and the phenomenal might
of our most awesome God. We get to call young people
to follow Jesus at a time when many of them have never
thought that this is even an option in their life. We get to
disciple and train the next generation of church leaders
and church planters in this unfolding century. We get to
see our ministry multiplied throughout a generation as the
teenagers we minister to go and spread this message with
ever-increasing impact.

How many young people are you in contact with now? 5?
50? 500? Even if you only have five in your youth ministry,
can you see how absolutely crucial that is? Because it's not
just these five lives that you will be impacting. The question
you have to ask is: *"How many people will these five*
young people influence throughout their lifetime?" Can you
see the enormous multiplication effect that your faithful
ministry can have? Can you see what it means to change a
generation?

What will become of your group members in the future?
Who knows? You have absolutely no idea of the influence
that some of those individuals might have. You are reaching
out to the future leaders of our nation. You are discipling
the future captains of industry and leaders of business. You
are working with rock stars before they become famous,
sports heroes before they become world champions,

political leaders long before they have even earned their first vote, judges before they have heard their first case, and internet entrepreneurs before they have accumulated their first million. You get to shape and mould our future artists, creators, performers, teachers, husbands, mothers, public servants, police, doctors, trades-people, activists, law-makers and factory workers.

Somewhere, someone invested time and ministry into the young lady we knew as Mother Teresa of Calcutta. Someone taught the Bible to Billy Graham when he was a lad. You simply do not know where God will lead those restless, fidgeting and difficult teenagers as he moulds them and shapes them and reveals to them their destiny.

All of us have a "use by" date. No one stays on this planet forever. **We get to raise a generation of kids who will be advancing God's kingdom long after we are dead and gone.** Indeed, the Christian church is always only one generation away from withering and dying. We get to sow into young people who will ensure that that day never arrives.

We are ministering to the most strategic group of people on the planet. We get to influence the 50% of the citizens of this world who are too young to vote. Remarkably, 85% of all people who will ever come to Christ do so before they reach their nineteenth birthday. We get to work with this strategic 85%.

In Matthew 20:1-16, Jesus tells the story of a man who hired workers at six in the morning. He then went back and got some more at nine. And at noon. And at three in the afternoon. He even hired some more men at five in the afternoon, just before knock-off time. When everyone finished at six, every single worker was given a full day's pay. (Praise God we have a master who gives us what we need, rather than what we deserve!)

By just extending this story a little, we realise what an amazing privilege it is to work with young people. **We get to train the workers who start at six in the morning!** Most young people who come to Christ have a whole lifetime—another 40 or 50 or 60 years of growing as a passionate disciple and being an active disciple-maker. What a fantastic privilege to work with them and prepare them for a lifetime of impactful ministry!

3. Four decisions of a generation-changer

As we read through David's words in Psalm 71, we see some significant attitudes and decisions displayed. What are the attitudes you need to develop and the decisions you need to make if you are indeed going to be a powerful generation-changer?

a) I will trust in you alone

In you, O LORD, I have taken refuge; let me never be put to shame. **Psalm 71:1**

There is the first decision of a generation-changer. You say to God: *"I will trust in you alone"*.

You need to be careful where you place your trust. You need to be careful where you take refuge or shelter. You need to make sure that the thing you take refuge in—your place of safety—is powerful enough to protect you.

If you're drowning at sea, there is no use clambering into a boat which is also sinking. If you shelter under a tree in a storm, you'd better be sure that no lightning is coming your way. If you're lost in the woods, then before you take refuge in a gingerbread cottage, you need to check out whether there is a wicked witch inside! You need to make sure that the thing you take refuge in—the person whom you trust—is powerful enough and willing enough to protect you.

In youth ministry it's easy to trust in some very shaky refuges. Sometimes you can trust in being part of a good church, or having a large youth ministry, or leading an awesome small group, or being dazzled with how God has gifted you, or being kept afloat by the admiration and applause of others. They all feel great, but they are very shaky refuges indeed!

I fell into this trap in my first position as a youth pastor. We had a senior-high youth group that consisted of about 25 enthusiastic students who would gather at my place each Friday night in the rumpus room out the back. It was great. It was wild. There was some solid spiritual growth. And my own spiritual journey? On fire as well!

It wasn't until the fourth year that I realised something was wrong. Suddenly, the group was not going as well. Numbers were dropping off. Enthusiasm levels were plummeting. There were a few students who walked right away from Jesus. A bit depressing, really.

But I then noticed something about my own relationship with Jesus. **It started to go downhill as well!** When I checked out what was going wrong, when I honestly confronted what was happening in my own personal life, I was challenged with a painful truth: **My own spiritual walk was dependent on how the youth group was going!** When the youth group went well—my journey as a Christian went well! But when the youth group was in the doldrums, my own personal relationship with Jesus headed in the same direction.

I was trusting in the wrong thing. I was taking refuge in the wrong place. I was trusting in the success of my own ministry to dictate how well I went as a Christian. A very shaky refuge indeed!

David says confidently: *"In you, O LORD, I have taken refuge"*.

And do you know the **result** of trusting everything to God?

*"In you, O LORD, I have taken refuge; **let me never be put to shame**."*

Now **that's** a good refuge! One where you will never be put to shame!

It's easy to live your life in the grip of shame. Especially if you're trusting in how you're going. Because you will always fail—one way or another, somewhere along the line. What is worse is that there will be no shortage of people to **remind** you that you have failed and to push you further and further down.

The devil himself will accuse you. "Look at what you've done! What right have you got to be a youth leader?" Your behaviour certainly does matter, and there may be some issues where you need to step aside from leadership while you sort them out. But if you keep dwelling on your past, you will always be in the pit of shame. The evil one will always try and get you to focus on your mistakes. But the faithful youth leader keeps their focus on Jesus and his death, because that is where their mistakes have been dealt with.

Jesus has dealt with your past—therefore you can have a great future!

If you are struggling on in your youth ministry life, ruled by shame, haunted by your failings—then come on, take refuge in your Lord and place your trust in him. Grab some trusted Christian friends and ask them to walk with you while you sort things out. The "blameless" person in the Bible isn't the one who is perfect—they are the person who is actively dealing with their sins and turning away from them.

And when you place your trust firmly in Jesus, then, along with David, you can say:

> *For you have been my hope, O Sovereign LORD, my confidence since my youth. From my birth I have relied on you; you brought me forth from my mother's womb. I will ever praise you.* **Psalm 71:5-6**

b) I will be a powerful example

> *I have become like a portent to many, but you are my strong refuge.* **Psalm 71:7**

The word "portent" is an odd word. It means a "sign", a "miracle", a "wonder".

God sometimes uses signs and wonders to accompany and authenticate his message. When God raised up Moses to confront Pharaoh so that he would release God's people from slavery in Egypt, God authenticated Moses' message with signs and wonders. When the apostles first took God's word to the Gentile world, we see many miracles and signs that backed up their message.

Often we become fascinated with these signs and wonders—and we'd love God to do them right in front of us. Sometimes we even demand it of God! (And get upset when it doesn't work out the way we want!)

And maybe God will do that sometimes. But in David's thinking, what is the "sign" or "portent" from God?

"I have become like a portent to many." David himself was that sign. As a leader, his life was the powerful example that backed up God's spoken word. If you are a leader, then you are that sign from God. You are the living evidence of the power of God to rescue people and change them to be his.

Don't be fooled. The eyes of a generation are on you. And to all sorts of hurting kids, you are a sign and an example. When they're trying to work out "What would Jesus do?", they will look at you. They want to see whether the way you live matches what you teach.

That's why spending time with kids is important. Have them over at your place. Allow them to see you doing "normal" things. They will see you deal with things well; they will see how you handle it when you fail. They will learn far more about how to respect their parents by seeing the way **you** treat **your** parents. They will learn far more about how to treat their spouse by seeing the way **you** interact with **your** husband or wife. They will learn how a Christian deals with anger by seeing **you** stuck in traffic or playing on the sporting field.

They will know that Jesus has the power to change them when they see that he is already changing you.

c) I will never give up

> *Do not cast me away when I am old; do not forsake*
> *me when my strength is gone.* **Psalm 71:9**

I meet many people who are involved in youth leadership. I go to conferences where there are stacks of youth pastors and volunteer leaders. But it is very hard to find a youth pastor who has been at their church for longer than three years. Yes, there they are—full of enthusiasm with a burning desire to invest into a generation so that together, "we can change the world"… but what happens to them all? I'm sure some of them think: *"I'll do ministry for a while until my life gets too busy"*; *"I'll do youth ministry until I mature"*; *"I'll hang out with students until something better comes along"*.

Okay—I understand that God will call some people to be in youth ministry for a short time while he prepares them for something else. But I want to challenge you. **How long will you stay in youth ministry?** We need some people to say: *"I'll do youth ministry as long as I have breath"*. We need parent-type figures in youth ministry. Every year as I have grown a little older (and a little greyer), youth ministry gets **easier**! Young people are far more likely to share with me the deep issues of their life now that I am near fifty, rather than when I was the gung-ho novice in my young twenties.

There are stacks of times when I have wanted to give up in youth ministry:

I rang all six students in my Bible-study group—all said they were coming—but only two arrived the next afternoon.

I organised the big youth-group night—everyone said they were bringing a friend—but "Little Miss Popular" had her birthday party the same night and 75% of our youth group abandoned our fantastic plans. I was left alone with half a dozen kids in a big empty hall with hundreds of cans of drink we could never sell and a $1000 loss on the night.

I had been growing with some students in a Bible-study group for a few years—we were close, we were supportive, it was a great group of high-school-aged disciples. Then, three of our group simply "gave up" on Jesus, and walked away completely. We were all devastated.

Young people have let me down. Leaders have let me down. Parents have let me down. Senior pastors have let me down. I have let myself down. If I'd been wanting to get out, I've had no shortage of opportunities. Yet in Psalm 71, David has a passion to be flat out for God even when he's old and grey. So, how long will **you** stay in youth ministry? Here is my challenge: *"Will you stay in youth ministry long enough to get good at it?"* (More about this in Chapter 18.)

I sometimes wonder what would happen if the medical profession were run the same way as youth ministry. That is, dedicated people went off and studied medicine for a number of years—but nobody ever practised as a doctor for longer than three years. After three years they all went off and did something else. Imagine if that happened right throughout the land! Let's now ask a few key questions:

a) Would our country have any doctors? Yes!
b) Would our country have any **good** doctors? No!

If nobody stayed at being a doctor for longer than three years, then no one would ever stay long enough to get good at it! And who would train the incoming batch of new doctors? **Someone who'd only done it for three years themselves!**

If you truly have a vision of being a generation-changer, then you need to start thinking about youth leadership **long-term**. You will never change a generation in an

18-month stint of leading the youth group at your local church! I never want to give up ministering for Jesus as long as I have breath!

David says:

> *But as for me, I shall always have hope; I will praise you more and more.* **Psalm 71:14**

What about you?

d) I will proclaim your righteousness alone
> *My mouth will tell of your righteousness, of your salvation all day long.* **Psalm 71:15**

If you truly want to be used by God to change a generation, then here is one issue that you simply must get right. It is God's righteousness that you are to proclaim. Not your own. Sure—you might be a helpful example to them, but in the end, you do not point students to yourself—you point them to God.

If it is **my** righteousness that I am proclaiming, then I am giving kids a hero who will ultimately crush them. Yes, I want to present myself as a model of how to be a Christian, but I also want to present myself as a model of a Christian who **fails**. I need to avoid the trap of presenting myself to our group as: "Mr Perfect, who gets everything right". They need to know that I struggle, and that sometimes I fall.

You might just be surprised at how "perfect" some teenagers will think you are!

John was 14. He was from a Christian family, but reasonably new at being a disciple in his own right. We had spent a bit of time together, and I was seeking to encourage him in his newly established faith. We got onto the issue of personal

Bible reading—you know, spending some individual time with Jesus and learning from his word. John was telling me how he was struggling in this area, and then he made this remarkable statement: *"I find it really hard to get to my Bible and read it. I wish I was like you, cos it's obvious that you do it really easily."*

I gasped. "Really easily"? Nothing could be further from the truth! I struggle so much in this area sometimes! And yet he had worked out that I must have been pretty close to perfection! I could have faked it and gone along with his idealistic misunderstanding: *"Sure, kid, when you're as good as me, you too can be a super-spiritual Christian!"* But we are not here to proclaim our own righteousness.

I told him my failings, we discussed how we could both encourage each other, and we looked to God and his righteousness as our encouragement.

If it is your righteousness that you are proclaiming, then you are giving teenagers a hero who will ultimately crush them.

Can you catch how passionate David is to tell of God's righteousness alone? (The emphasis is mine!)

*My mouth will tell of **your** righteousness, of **your** salvation all day long, though I know not its measure. I will come and proclaim **your** mighty acts, O Sovereign LORD; I will proclaim **your** righteousness, yours alone. Since my youth, O God, you have taught me, and to this day I declare **your** marvellous deeds. Even when I am old and grey, do not forsake me, O God, till I declare **your** power to the next generation, **your** might to all who are to come. **Psalm 71:15-18**

And do you know why it really matters that we focus on God's righteousness alone?

> *Your righteousness reaches to the skies, O God, you who have done great things. Who, O God, is like you? Though you have made me see troubles, many and bitter, you will restore my life again; from the depths of the earth you will again bring me up. You will increase my honour and comfort me once again.*
>
> **Psalm 71:19-21**

Are you seeing a few troubles in your life right now? Are things sometimes a little bitter for you? Hang in there! God will restore your life again—he will bring you up—he will increase your honour and comfort you once again.

These are the four decisions of a generation-changer:

> *"I will trust in you alone."*
>
> *"I will be a powerful example."*
>
> *"I will never give up."*
>
> *"I will proclaim your righteousness alone."*

Are you prepared to make these decisions? Are you prepared to make the sacrifices that are necessary to live out these decisions in your life? Do you have a commitment to God that draws you into a deep, personal and ongoing relationship with him? Do you have a vision that is big enough to see a whole generation changed for Jesus?

Can you say with David:

> *Even when I am old and grey, do not forsake me, O God, till I declare your power to the next generation, your might to all who are to come.*   **Psalm 71:18**

You are a generation-changer!

Chapter 3
You are a shepherd

There are many pictures in the Bible to describe a Christian leader. But for me, two great pictures stand out. The first picture describes a leader as a "shepherd"; the second describes a leader as a "servant".

We often call the leader of a church a "pastor" or "minister". These popular titles that we give to Christian leaders come from these two pictures. The word "pastor" means "shepherd"; the word "minister" means "servant".

We will look at what it means to be a "servant-leader" in Chapter 6. Right now, let's focus on what it means to be a "shepherd-leader".

1. Your view of a shepherd

Close your eyes for a moment... go on, give it a try... I want you to imagine what picture comes into your mind when I say the word "shepherd". Go on—close your eyes now and visualise this for a moment. Got it? What did you see?

Some of you may have come up with a picture of a bronzed and craggy Aussie sheep farmer with squillions of acres of dry and dusty land, where thousands of dirty, woolly sheep gambol across never-ending paddocks. Perhaps you can "see" the farmer on his tractor... or his motorbike... or his horse... or even his helicopter... aided and abetted by his faithful dogs... rounding up enough sheep to keep roasts on the table well into the next century.

Or maybe you "saw" a different picture. Perhaps you imagined a more "ancient" shepherd from times gone by. Perhaps you had to play the part of a shepherd in your kindergarten's nativity play, and you've never lived it down since. The shepherd in this picture wears a wrap-around sheet, a beach towel on his head, holds a crooked stick in his right hand, and lovingly carries a few weak lambs who "baa" at him with love and devotion.

What sort of picture did you "see" when you thought of the image of a "shepherd"?

The biblical picture of a shepherd is a very strong one. Not only is it a key image used to describe the ministry of Jesus, it is also one of the most common descriptions of anyone who is a leader in God's congregation. If you are a youth leader—or any other sort of Christian leader—then you need to understand what it means to be a shepherd.

2. God's view of a shepherd

In the Old Testament there is a quick snapshot which shows us God's picture of a shepherd. It is a description of one of the greatest leaders of the Old Testament—indeed, one of the greatest shepherds of the Old Testament. We are given a quick summary of how God appointed David to be one of his key leaders. God gives us an important lesson which shows us how to be great youth leaders.

> *He chose David his servant and took him from the*
> *sheep pens; from tending the sheep he brought him*
> *to be the shepherd of his people Jacob, of Israel*
> *his inheritance. And David shepherded them with*
> *integrity of heart; with skilful hands he led them.*
> **Psalms 78:70-72**

There's a mountain of information in those three small verses. Let's have a quick look!

a) God chooses

"He chose David."

This is God's world; we are his sheep; he chooses his shepherds. Make sense?

If there's a farmer who owns a large sheep station or ranch, then he owns the sheep as well. And if he owns the sheep, then he must choose the shepherds. The shepherds are on his team—and they work under his direction. That's the way life on the land works. The owner chooses the shepherds. **The shepherds don't choose themselves, and they are not elected by a popular vote from the sheep!**

Every Christian group will have different methods for appointing their leaders. We all need to make sure that we have a system that keeps us accountable before God. Maybe you're a youth leader "because you wanted to be"; maybe you're a youth leader "because the pastor asked you"; maybe you even got voted into the position. But in God's eyes you are a leader, you are a shepherd—because God himself chooses you. You are on God's team, and you work under his direction. Ultimately you will answer to God for how you fulfil your job as a shepherd on his team.

So… don't promote yourself to be a youth leader. Check out with trusted Christian friends whether you really feel that God himself is choosing you.

b) We serve

"He chose David his servant."

A person who is a Christian leader is primarily a servant. God raises you up so that you might serve him, and serve those whom he has placed around you. We often tend to think of leaders being "the boss", but Jesus himself sets the example of being a servant.

What was David doing when God chose him to be a leader over his people? He was out looking after the sheep. He was getting them their food and cleaning out their mess. He was doing the job of a servant. If you want to be a **leader** in God's church, then you need to start out by being a **servant**. *(Jesus said something like that in Mark 10:43!)*

Shaun was a 15-year-old loosely associated with our church. He showed up on Sunday mornings with his family, but he never got involved in anything else. One day he said to me proudly: *"I'm going to be a Sunday-school teacher!"*

Inwardly I groaned. As far as I could work out, Shaun didn't even have a living faith in Jesus. Why on earth would he take on a ministry position in his local church? However, I tried to respond with enthusiasm to Shaun, who was bursting at the seams with pride.

"Wow—what made you decide you wanted to be a Sunday School teacher?"

"I just can't wait to boss the little kids around!"

Ouch! Something about being a servant got completely lost in that transaction. If you're becoming a youth leader because you want to be "in charge", please back off right away. **God not only chooses whom he will have as his**

shepherds, but he chooses people who are prepared to be servants.

c) God promotes

"...and took him from the sheep pens; from tending the sheep he brought him to be the shepherd of his people Jacob."

David was already a shepherd—being faithful in tending his family's sheep. Not only did God call him and choose him, it was God who also promoted him. It was God who gave him a much more significant sheepfold to look after—Jacob, his own people, his own inheritance, his own nation of Israel. David did not promote himself. If the job was being offered, he probably wouldn't have even applied. It was God who said:

"You are doing a faithful job as a servant in tending the family sheep. That's the sort of faithfulness I want in someone to shepherd my whole nation."

Brad was a good youth leader. But he would look enviously at other leaders at other churches that had bigger youth groups. He used to look around the fifteen or so teenagers who would meet in his lounge-room and feel that his own work was so insignificant. If only he could be the leader of a much larger and more successful youth group! Then he'd really be someone important! So he started making plans to try and leave his own youth group, and become a leader in a bigger and better one.

Do not despise the day of small things! If God has called you to lead only a handful of students, then rejoice in that and be faithful. What God is looking for is the heart of a servant.

Then he will entrust us with bigger things. It is God himself who does the "promoting".

d) The two requirements of a shepherd

"And David shepherded them with integrity of heart; with skilful hands he led them."

Did you catch the two requirements for a shepherd? Did you catch the two things that God expected of David in his leadership? Did you catch the two things that God expects of you in your leadership?

Integrity of Heart... AND... Skilful Hands

That's it! Only two things you've got to achieve to be a faithful shepherd! Integrity of heart... and... skilful hands. What could be simpler?

You know that each of these can be kind of tricky to achieve. Even the great King David stumbled a few times in these areas. And yet the Bible is full of instruction as to how you can achieve this. God himself wants you to be a faithful shepherd—and he will give you all the instruction and training you need so you can be the leader that he has designed you to be.

"Integrity of heart" has to do with your **relationships**, and "skilful hands" has to do with your **tasks**. We'll learn more about these key relationships in Chapter 4, and more about these key tasks in Chapter 5.

Chapter 4

Three relationships of a shepherd

The New Testament view of a shepherd

You probably know the word "pastor". It's often used to describe a leadership position in the church. Sometimes it only refers to the senior leadership position in a church. Some churches will use words like "minister", "rector", "priest" and a whole variety of others, but most of us know what the role of a "pastor" is.

Or do we? The word "pastor" is only used once in the NIV New Testament (Ephesians 4:11). However, **the word for "pastor" is exactly the same Greek word as "shepherd"**. So if we want to find out the biblical role of a "pastor" or "shepherd", then we can check out what the New Testament says about that very role. And if you are a youth leader, you too are a shepherd—or a pastor—and so these words also apply to you.

If you research the whole of the New Testament—and look up every reference to "shepherd"—you will discover two amazing things. Firstly, there are only **three key relationships** for a shepherd. Secondly, there are only three key tasks of a shepherd.

That's right! If you understand these three relationships, and know these three tasks, you are well on your way to being a faithful shepherd. You are well on your way to being a good pastor. You are well on your way to being a fantastic youth leader.

Read on!

If you want to maintain your "integrity of heart", then you need to be strong in your key relationships. Throughout the whole of the New Testament there are three key relationships for anyone who wants to be a faithful shepherd. These are three absolutely crucial relationships for any youth leader!

Relationship 1: Know Jesus, your Shepherd

The first relationship of any shepherd—or pastor (remember, the words mean the same thing)—is to realise that we are only under-shepherds. That is, each one of us already has our own shepherd—Jesus himself. He calls each one of us to follow him—he calls each one of us into a close and loving relationship. He leads us in the paths we should follow, and he calls us to obey him and trust him. He reaches out with his rod of correction when we stray from his path, and he binds up our wounds and carries us along when we need his help.

This is such a huge relationship! Look at how much it means to have Jesus as your shepherd.

a) He is your king who gives you life

For the Lamb at the centre of the throne will be their shepherd; he will lead them to springs of living water.

Revelation 7:17

Can you picture Jesus—your shepherd—who is your king upon his heavenly throne? He is calling you to worship him. What a privilege!

I tend to forget this side of things. I just rush around doing ministry after ministry, running programme after programme. Sometimes I can be so busy making sure I'm doing "the work of the Lord" that I forget all about "the Lord of the work". Long before Jesus wants you to be a shepherd and a leader, he wants you to be a worshipper. In public. And in private. Is he calling you to his throne now? Well, put this book down, and go and hang out with him for a while. We will still be here when you come back! Go on!

Back so soon? Yeah—I'm a bit like that, too. I think that I neglect being a faithful worshipper of Jesus because it seems like "down" time. You know—nothing practical will be achieved. But have a look again at the verse from Revelation. What does this "shepherd" on the throne do for us? When he calls us to gather around him, he will: *"lead us to springs of living water"* (that's what shepherds do!)

When I worship Jesus **I will be refreshed**! Yee-hah! And I can tell you—after three decades as a full-time, front-line youth pastor— **you're going to need stacks of refreshment**, be assured of that!

Oh, it is a marvellous thing to have Jesus as your shepherd!

b) He is your guide who calls you back

For you were like sheep going astray, but now you have returned to the Shepherd and Overseer of your souls.   ***1 Peter 2:25***

Another great thing about having Jesus as our shepherd is that he keeps us on the path that God has designed for us. He not only shows us the path, he not only walks ahead of us and clears the way, but he also grabs hold of us when we wander away and calls us back to follow him (that's what shepherds do!)

What's this got to do with being a good youth leader? Very simply, most youth leaders who "wander away" do so at this point. Most don't give up on ministry because they didn't have enough skills. Most who give up do so because they're not prepared to stay on the path that God has planned. What would it take to drag you away from following Jesus? A career path… success at your chosen endeavour… popularity… a sexual relationship… apathy… What would it take to drag you away?

Having Jesus as my shepherd means he will call me back. And, man, I **hate** it when he does that! And I **never** feel like stopping what I'm doing, and giving up something that's sinful!

But I know he wants to refresh me. I know he wants what's best for me. So if you want to maintain your "integrity of heart", then it doesn't mean that you'll always be perfect. But it does mean that you will be honest about when you're wandering away, and you'll come back with true repentance.

c) He is your God who rewards you

> *Be shepherds of God's flock … And when the Chief Shepherd appears, you will receive the crown of glory that will never fade away.*   *1 Peter 5:2, 4*

It's natural to look for rewards. It's so satisfying when someone acknowledges that you're doing a great job. Students look for the rewards of the honour roll; sports people long for the trophy which says "Champion"; all of us love it when someone reaches out and says: *"You're doing well! Keep it up!"*

Sometimes the rewards are hard to find in youth ministry. We are dealing with growing adolescents who might not show the results of our hard labour for many years. We are ministering to fragile teenagers who probably aren't the most affirming people in the world. Sometimes it can be very discouraging.

Where do we get our rewards from? Hopefully they will come from the community of leaders that we belong to—and from those who oversee and supervise our work. Sometimes, our rewards will come directly from the students that we minister with—as we see the work of God changing their lives for eternity.

But sometimes you might feel very unaffirmed. Discouraged. Disheartened. Wondering whether it is all worth it. I think I understand these feelings all too well!

If you're feeling a bit down, you might find the temptation to go and look for **your own rewards**. Perhaps a spirit of competition will enter into what you do. You might bust your boiler to try and prove that you are a better youth leader than all the others at your church (or certainly better than what's happening at the church down the road!) Or maybe you will draw in your group members way too close—because **you** feel good when you're relating to them, and they end up serving **your** needs. Or maybe you will seek your rewards by doing something that is wrong... something that bends the rules *just a little bit*... something that lies way outside what Jesus would approve of... because you simply want to feel good—and fast.

This is a dangerous road. A road that will take you away from "integrity of heart". And yet God himself provides the answers.

If you strengthen your relationship with Jesus, if you bow before him as your great shepherd, if you realise that you are serving under his rule and his authority, then you will also realise **he is the one who rewards you**. He knows what you need, he knows what you're feeling, and he will look after you.

So, keep being faithful in ministry all your life, keep working hard at strengthening your relationship with Jesus, keep being determined to maintain a heart of integrity. And then, having seen the fruit of a faithful ministry, won't it be a great day *"when the Chief Shepherd appears, and you will receive the crown of glory that will never fade away"*?!

There's the first key relationship for any pastor, or shepherd, or leader. **Know Jesus, your shepherd.** That's where everything else starts.

Relationship 2: Know your heart

To be a faithful New Testament pastor (or shepherd), you also need to "know yourself". You need to know your own heart. You need to be aware of your own areas of weakness, and to guard your heart so that you do not stray from the path that Jesus has designed for you.

There are three dangers for shepherds that the New Testament warns us about:

a) The danger of pretending

Watch out for false prophets. They come to you in sheep's clothing, but inwardly they are ferocious wolves.   **Matthew 7:15**

The Bible is full of warnings for shepherds who are only pretending to care for the sheep. You have probably heard stories of youth leaders or other pastors who have been caught helping themselves. Perhaps their hand was in the till. Perhaps they were caught with their pants down. Maybe they just wanted all the glory for themselves. Maybe they were power hungry.

A good friend of mine was a youth pastor on the other side of town. A vibrant youth ministry in a growing church. He had an assistant youth pastor who looked after the junior high area. The church was blown apart and the youth ministry destroyed when his assistant was convicted of committing acts of indecency against two 14-year-old boys. *"They come to you in sheep's clothing, but inwardly they are ferocious wolves."*

I know what you're saying: *"That could never happen to me. I would never do anything like that."* And I believe you. But be aware. That assistant youth pastor I mentioned above, who was sentenced to 18 months jail, was once a respected leader in a thriving youth ministry, and he too probably said: *"That could never happen to me. I would never do anything like that."*

If you're going to be a faithful shepherd, then you need to know your own heart. You need to know how easy it is to satisfy your own needs. As a Christian leader, you need to be aware of the danger of pretending.

b) The danger of having no substance
These men are blemishes at your love feasts, eating with you without the slightest qualm—shepherds who feed only themselves. They are clouds without rain, blown along by the wind; autumn trees, without fruit and uprooted—twice dead.   ***Jude 1:12***

There are some chilling descriptions of leaders in this passage.

i. "Shepherds who only feed themselves"
The shepherd's job is to feed his sheep. That means he must guide them to green pastures, and lead them to drink from clear water. The pastor's job is exactly the same. We are to guide God's people to whatever will grow them as strong disciples.

Imagine a scene where a shepherd guides his sheep to green pastures, but before any of them can feed, he goes around himself and eats every speck of grass! Ridiculous! Equally ridiculous is the notion that a Christian pastor could be more interested in furthering his own career or reputation, rather than genuinely helping his flock!

But it happens. You might find yourself in youth ministry primarily because it is meeting **your** needs. Making you feel wanted, making you feel liked, enjoying the acceptance of young people when your own relationships with other adults are awkward.

You need to know your own heart. Think about your youth leadership and the assessment that others will make of it. Could you ever be described as a *"shepherd who only feeds himself"*?

ii. "Clouds without rain, blown along by the wind"
Imagine this scene in the Australian outback. The land is in drought. No rain has been seen for months. Your farming land is cracked and dried. Time is running out for this season's crop. If it doesn't rain soon, your crop will be ruined and your livelihood devastated.

And then on the horizon, you see a beautiful sign. Clouds are gathering, and being blown in your direction. You gather the whole family—watching in amazement as the sky fills with thick clouds. You are ready to celebrate once those first drops start falling on the parched earth. Anticipation is high. This is the moment you have been waiting for.

But no rain comes. The clouds appear—they look promising—but they just keep being blown by the wind without delivering their promised refreshment. The clouds just blow away to reveal a clear sky and a continued drought. They were just *"clouds without rain, blown along by the wind"*.

Can you imagine being a shepherd like that? Can you imagine being a leader like that? Everyone sees you arrive—you are full of promise as to what you will deliver—this is going to be a revolution in youth ministry. You talk about the rich outpouring of God's Spirit on dry and desolate lives and everyone is excited by the bountiful harvest that will result.

But it is all talk. It is all show. The programmes might look great, your activities might look exciting, even the music might be awesome—but there is no substance. There is no mighty move of God behind this. It is all smoke and mirrors. Signs and wonders. But there is no blessing from God—there is no reality behind the promises—it's just an exciting youth programme that does not deliver blessing to anyone's life, and there is no abundant harvest that follows.

The kids were excited, the leaders were excited, the church was excited. But God's hand was not in it, and everyone walks away with heavy hearts.

You need to know your own heart. Think about your youth leadership and the assessment that others will make of it. Could you ever be described as *"clouds without rain, blown along by the wind"*? *"Autumn trees, without fruit and uprooted—twice dead"*?

This is the same idea, with a different picture. Leadership is meant to be like a fruitful tree. You give life—you give growth—and there is an abundant harvest in the lives of the young people that you touch. As God's shepherd, you are there to produce "fruit that will last". *(Can I recommend a great book by that name?!)*

But picture an autumn tree—where the leaves which were full of life have already fallen to the ground. Picture a tree that is barren and fruitless. Not achieving what a tree is meant to achieve. It is already "dead". But now imagine the same tree, pulled out of the ground and completely uprooted: "twice dead".

In any form of Christian leadership there is the danger of not delivering what you promise. Of not keeping your word. Of letting down a teenager who had pinned their hopes on you.

You need to know your own heart. Think about your youth leadership and the assessment that others will make of it. Could you ever be described as *"autumn trees, without fruit and uprooted—twice dead"*?

c) The danger of wrong motives
Be shepherds of God's flock that is under your care, serving as overseers—not because you must, but because you are willing, as God wants you to be; not greedy for money, but eager to serve; not lording it

> *over those entrusted to you, but being examples to the*
> *flock.*   ***1 Peter 5:2-3***

Sometimes, youth leaders can end up doing all the **right** things for the **wrong** reasons. While this might look good on the outside, doing things for the wrong reasons will never bring glory to God, and will never result in a fruitful, lasting ministry.

There are three checkpoints given in the above Bible passage:

i. Not because you have to, but because you want to

Maybe you're a youth leader "because someone had to do it". Perhaps you're there because of a strong sense of duty. Congratulations! This sort of commitment is to be admired! The world would be a better place if more people took their responsibilities seriously!

But if you're a youth leader **only** "because you have to", there is something missing. If you're only leading youth out of a strong sense of duty, there is a whole dimension that is absent. The picture of a shepherd in the Bible is of someone who **loves their sheep and loves looking after them**. Can you honestly say that about the young people that you lead? *"I love my group and I love caring for them."*

If God has truly called you to lead in youth ministry, then he will give you the desire to do it. If you're just doing it because you have to, there will be no joy in what you do, and you'll find that either your students burn out, or **you** burn out really quickly!

ii. Not greedy for gain, but eager to serve

The text actually says, *"not greedy for money"*. I must admit I don't know of many church youth leaders who are making much money out of the deal, but you certainly can be greedy for other things: popularity; acceptance; status; recognition. Enough said.

The essence of being a shepherd is to **serve**. You exist for the sake of the sheep. You do whatever it takes so that they grow and prosper. If needed, you would give up your life for your sheep. *(This is what Jesus did!—John 10:11.)*

So do a quick check. Are you a youth leader because of what **you** will gain out of it, or are you there for what your **young people** will gain out of it?

iii. Not bossing others around, but being an example

The style of leadership that Jesus brought to us is completely different from the way most of the world operates. Have a listen in as Jesus chats with his disciples:

> Jesus called them together and said, "You know that those who are regarded as rulers of the Gentiles lord it over them, and their high officials exercise authority over them. Not so with you. Instead, whoever wants to become great among you must be your servant, and whoever wants to be first must be slave of all."
>
> **Mark 10:42-44**

Jesus talks about the normal style of leadership where: *"the rulers of the Gentiles lord it over them"*. You're probably very familiar with this style of leadership. It's the leadership of "bosses" and "workers". You lead by separation. The managers of the factory floor will have air-conditioned offices high above the noisy production line. Officers on a naval vessel will live on a separate deck from the enlisted sailors. A business executive will have a large and intimidating desk just to remind you who's the boss! Teachers at a school will have privileges that students can never enjoy.

Maybe there is a place for this style of leadership in the world. Perhaps this separation is needed to make things work. But don't confuse Christian leadership with this. Jesus never operated this way. He didn't hang onto his exalted status as the Son of God and claim privileges for himself above the common people of his day. He didn't direct his mission to Planet Earth from the 42nd floor of an air-conditioned hotel in a flashy city. He was born as a peasant in a cultural backwater, and lived among a people who were oppressed by the Roman occupation. He lived and suffered and died in a brutal world with no executive perks or frequent-flyer points. **He led by example.** As the very next verse says in Mark 10:

> *For even the Son of Man did not come to be served,*
> *but to serve, and to give his life as a ransom for*
> *many.*   ***Mark 10:45***

That is the role of a shepherd. Avoid the danger of just "being the boss", and lead by example. If you want to lead with integrity of heart, then you need to know your own heart, and avoid the danger of doing right things for the wrong motives.

Relationship 3: Know your sheep

The man who enters by the gate is the shepherd of his sheep. The watchman opens the gate for him, and the sheep listen to his voice. He calls his own sheep by name and leads them out. When he has brought out all his own, he goes on ahead of them, and his sheep follow him because they know his voice. **John 10:2-4**

Do you get a feel of the relationship between the shepherd and his sheep? This is no distant farmer rolling by uncaringly on his tractor. This is a shepherd who knows every sheep individually and cares for every sheep individually.

"He calls his own sheep by name."

"His sheep follow him because they know his voice."

This is the third key relationship for any shepherd. This is the third key relationship for any leader. As well as knowing Jesus, your own shepherd (and the **huge** blessings which that brings); as well as knowing your own heart (and the dangers which that brings); you also need to know your own sheep. Deeply. Individually. Lovingly.

"Hang on! What if I have a youth group of 300 teenagers?"

I wrestle with this one myself. Anyone who knows me will tell you that remembering names is not one of my strengths. There is **no way** that I know every single one of the students who show up at *Crossfire* on an average night. If truth be told, I can't always get the names right for every one of my 100 youth leaders!

But the principle still holds. **I expect that every teenager who belongs to our Crossfire community will be well known by at least one of our leaders.** And I expect that every single one of our leaders will be loved and cared for by one of our team leaders or co-ordinators. And I expect that every one of our team leaders or co-ordinators will be cared for individually by one of my staff team. My role? **I need to care deeply and individually for each person on my staff team.** So even in a big ministry, the principle still holds. The third key relationship for a faithful New Testament shepherd is: "Know Your Sheep".

This relationship really matters. Ministry is always about people. Individual people. Special people with their own unique circumstances and needs. Not everyone will fit your ministry system. But everyone matters. If a young person comes along to your youth ministry, will they leave at the end of the night and feel that they were loved and cared for? If you have a team of New Testament shepherds as your leaders, then this can be achieved—and your ministry should be fruitful. But if you have leaders who are *"shepherds who feed only themselves ... clouds without rain ... autumn trees, without fruit and uprooted—twice dead"*, then you will just have an interesting programme which churns through a set number of kids each night.

It is a huge privilege to be a shepherd on God's team. As a youth leader, you need to understand that this is your role. To be effective as a shepherd, you need to maintain "integrity of heart". You do this by focusing on three key relationships—to know Jesus, your own shepherd; to know your heart; and to know your sheep.

Once you have these three relationships working, what are you meant to do? What are the **tasks** of a New Testament shepherd? You will be pleased to know that there are only three things that the New Testament tells you to do.

More about this in the next chapter!

Chapter 5
Three tasks of a shepherd

It can be confusing to be a youth leader. There are so many things to do! There are young people to be contacted, activities to be organised, games to be run, food to be ordered, Bible studies to be prepared, kids who need to be listened to, equipment to be set up, rubbish to be emptied, halls to be cleaned, broken windows to be fixed... and of course there are parents who want little Johnny looked after, and pastors who want their youth ministry to go well... not to mention your own personal life, work life, study life, home life, family life and everything else that demands attention from you! Sometimes it can all seem too much!

Relax. Take a few deep breaths. It will be okay. **The New Testament only spells out three tasks that a shepherd (or pastor) needs to get done!** If the key to "integrity of heart" is to get your relationships right, then the key to "skilful" hands is to simply get these three tasks right.

Just three things? Yep—three things! I scoured the whole of the New Testament to find out everything it says to shepherds—and I can only find three things that you really need to make sure that you do well.

Let's check it out!

Task 1: Find your sheep

As you read the New Testament, you quickly discover that a key element of being a shepherd is to have a heart for those sheep who are lost. The biblical shepherd does not just continue on with whatever sheep might follow him—they have a real heart and a real care for those sheep who are not yet with him. Those sheep who are refusing to follow. Those sheep who have wandered away. Those sheep who will not come.

a) Jesus' heart for the outsiders

Jesus experienced all this as he led his people. He wept over those who would not come and embrace the security and intimacy of the eternal relationship he was offering.

> *O Jerusalem, Jerusalem, you who kill the prophets*
> *and stone those sent to you, how often I have longed*
> *to gather your children together, as a hen gathers her*
> *chicks under her wings, but you were not willing!*
>
> **Luke 13:34**

When Jesus was accused of hanging out with the wrong crowd, he made it clear that he wasn't just interested in hanging around the religious insiders. He wanted to find those who realised their inner need for his spiritual forgiveness and healing.

> *But the Pharisees and the teachers of the law who*
> *belonged to their sect complained to his disciples,*
> *"Why do you eat and drink with tax collectors and*
> *'sinners'?" Jesus answered them, "It is not the healthy*
> *who need a doctor, but the sick. I have not come to*
> *call the righteous, but sinners to repentance."*
>
> **Luke 5:30-32**

Jesus didn't just lead the sheep who happened to join up with his gang. As a shepherd, he **intentionally** went to the outsiders—to the lost—to those who appeared to have no interest in him. As a shepherd, we see that Jesus had a huge impact on many who had been written off by the established church.

b) Our heart for the outsiders
When Jesus calls us to be shepherds, he calls us to have the same heart for the outsiders as he had. He calls us to the first task of a shepherd—to "find your sheep".

> *Suppose one of you has a hundred sheep and loses one of them. Does he not leave the ninety-nine in the open country and go after the lost sheep until he finds it? And when he finds it, he joyfully puts it on his shoulders and goes home. Then he calls his friends and neighbours together and says, "Rejoice with me; I have found my lost sheep." I tell you that in the same way there will be more rejoicing in heaven over one sinner who repents than over ninety-nine righteous persons who do not need to repent.* **Luke 15:4-7**

Jesus calls us to be shepherds who intentionally go and search for those sheep who have wandered. That's what Jesus did.

c) The youth leader as shepherd
Being a youth leader is no easy task. You can have a real mixture of kids—some who want to go where you're going, and others who appear to have no interest at all. Let me give you a quick outline of three very key groups of young people whom you need to keep in mind as you exercise your ministry.

i. The keen insiders

This first group of teenagers are the great ones to have around. These are young people who are absolutely with you all the way. Enthusiastic. Keen. Co-operative. And spiritual! Hanging on your every word. Growing as keen disciples. Standing up for Jesus. Leadership material. Ahh—youth ministry can be so easy with group members like this. So satisfying. So comfortable.

ii. The unresponsive attenders

Then there are the teenagers who make your life hell. They come along, but they're not interested. They wreck your programmes. They behave badly. They come forward at every altar call, but they never last as an obedient Christian for longer than about three hours. They giggle at inappropriate points in your sermon, and commit serious acts of flatulence during quiet prayer. They never listen— they're never doing what everyone in the group is meant to be doing, and when you challenge them, they reply with: *"You're so unfair! You're always picking on me!"* Very quietly you wish that they'd start attending the youth group at the church down the road instead of yours. (In fact, in an exasperated moment, you may have even **suggested** this idea to them!)

iii. The unknown outsiders

There is a third group whom you may well overlook if you're not careful. They are the teenagers who currently have nothing to do with any of your ministries at all. They might attend the schools where your own young people go, they might live and work and shop and relax in your community, but they don't come to any activity you run. They're not part of your church at all. You never see them.

While you can easily overlook this third group, keep these key points in mind:

• *They are the largest group of young people in your community.*

• *They are the most needful of your church's ministry.*

• *They are where the growth of the church will come from.*

• *They are right at the heart of Jesus' ministry.*

Of course you may well have a ministry that **starts** with teenagers in the first group (The keen insiders). *(See my book Fruit That Will Last for a detailed explanation as to **why** this is good strategy.)* But if you **only** have a ministry to young people in this group, then you have a comfortable clubhouse, and you are a long way from the heart of Jesus who *"came to seek and to save [those who are] lost"* (Luke 19:10).

Similarly, if you are managing to attract teenagers from the second group (The unresponsive attenders), you may well feel like you are having a good outreach ministry. But if you neglect to reach out to the young people in the third group, (The unknown outsiders), then you have not picked up on the key task of a shepherd—to "find your sheep".

d) The problem with Little Bo Peep

One of the difficulties for youth leaders is finding the right role model. If you've moved into a youth ministry which has been a comfortable club for insiders for long enough, then you might have no model of how to put it right.

Somewhere along the line, Jesus has lost his "top spot" of being a role model for spiritual shepherds. His place has been usurped by a mischievous intruder. Jesus has been replaced by a person who has damaged the Christian church for centuries and must surely carry a substantial proportion of the blame for ineffective ministry throughout the ages.

Ladies and gentlemen, I am referring to none other than that evil shepherdess, Little Bo Peep. She has been the role model for pastors and youth leaders for too long, which has resulted in ministries that have failed to achieve the first task of shepherd—to find their sheep.

Read again those familiar words from the "Bo Peep Chronicles":

Little Bo Peep has lost her sheep
And doesn't know where to find them.

Okay, let's cut her some slack. Every shepherd has their off day. She was given a group of sheep to look after, **and she's lost them!** (Shame… shame… shame.) But have you ever had one of those days? You're leading a group of kids on a camp—when you went canoeing you know you had seven students. **Now you're back you can only find six!** Or maybe your youth group used to have fifty teenagers—now you have twelve kids and a couple of assorted dogs (on a good night). We all lose some sheep from time to time.

But look at the evil vixen's response to the desperate situation. How does Bo deal with the fact she has lost her sheep?

Leave them alone and they will come home
Wagging their tails behind them.

What sort of a ministry strategy is this? *"Leave them alone and they will come home"*? I suspect that if **you** were employing Bo to look after your sheep, with that sort of attitude, you would give her the sack, quick smart! Certainly if she were your babysitter, and she displayed the same attitude, you would terminate her employment immediately (and report her to the police for wilful neglect of a minor).

Unfortunately, many youth ministries have inherited the Little Bo Peep model of outreach: *"Leave them alone and they will come home"*.

Somehow we think that if we can just make the youth group **good** enough, if our activities are **interesting** enough, if our **sermons** are dynamic enough, if our Christian music is **loud** enough, then those who are outside Christ and his amazing love will mysteriously bring themselves home and plant themselves in his kingdom as growing disciples.

The heart of Jesus, the good shepherd, was *"to seek and to save those who are lost"*. The heart of a modern-day spiritual shepherd is no different. The first task of a New Testament shepherd or pastor is to "find their sheep".

e) The problem with religious Rambos
A word of warning. "Finding your sheep" isn't like Rambo finding a group of prisoners-of-war and rescuing them single-handedly and leading them home triumphantly.

When I first started in youth ministry, I guess I thought of myself that way. What glory there would be when I went where no youth pastor had dared to go, and approached the unapproachable, achieved the unachievable, redeemed the unredeemable, and restored the unrestorable!

Hmm. Way too many action movies in my life?

I have seen too many youth pastors abandon their work with the boring "church kids" and go off into the exotic realms of pagan-land to encounter the fierce savages lurking in outer darkness (or, at least, playing in the local school yard). This misunderstanding of their role has lead to real problems back at their church, and often led to unhappy and brief ministries!

Yes, "finding your sheep" is a vital role for a shepherd, but can I suggest three cautions?

i. Ministry is a team effort

The biblical emphasis is that the Christian congregation works **together** to achieve ministry. If you just go off by yourself to save the world, then you are missing the vital aspect of involving other members of the body in this ministry. So, just before you abandon the young people who are already at church so that you can go and save the masses, please keep the following in mind...

ii. Teenagers are best reached by other teenagers

If you have the genuine heart of a shepherd—if you have a Christlike heart for the lost—then you will use the outreach method that is most effective. And who is a 14-year-old most likely to listen to? A famous sports-star who has become a Christian? A gallant local church youth pastor? Both are helpful—but the most likely person to influence him is his 14-year-old friend. **The best way to reach out to students who are outside of Christ is to equip and inspire your Christian students to have a ministry to their friends.** This is "multiplication" ministry. Just going and doing it all yourself is "addition" ministry.

iii. So start by growing your Christian teenagers

If you want to reach the maximum number of youth possible—if you want to reach young people who are way outside the saving love of Jesus—then start by growing the small number of Christian teenagers that you already have. My book *Fruit That Will Last* outlines a complete strategy of how to do this. (I recommend you read this!)

Here is a quick story from *Fruit That Will Last*:

> *I made this mistake at a church once. We had a "keep going as we are" older youth ministry (young adults). We had about half a dozen high-schoolers who attended a Sunday morning programme. I had established an outreach at the local state high school and was developing good relationships with non-Christian students. Many were asking questions. I wanted an evangelistic group I could invite them to. I wanted to see them won to Christ's kingdom and implanted in his church.*
>
> *I grabbed our young adult group and asked: "who will lead?" A handful of enthusiastic helpers responded. I grabbed our six Christian high-schoolers. "Would you come? Would you bring your friends?" They said they'd check it out. I stood up at the local high-school assembly and announced our new youth group, and invited one and all to show up.*
>
> *Thirty non-Christian teenagers showed up the first night. Our six Christian kids were never to be seen after this point! Forty non-Christians came on the second night. Fifty on the third. It was wild! It was chaotic! It was out of control! The behaviour was uncontrollable. We could not enforce a reasonable*

*standard of discipline. Leaders were attacked with
rocks. Fights developed. The police had to be called.*

*I should say that in the middle of this chaos, one or
two teenagers decided to follow Jesus. But the cost
was too high. Many leaders were burned. The "nice"
kids stayed away—it was too wild for them. We
wanted to befriend these kids—instead we became
their disciplinarians.*

*I learned a strong lesson from this. **Don't start solo
with evangelism!** Build your ministry team and
disciple your Christian young people first. As you sow
into them a passion and a heart to see their friends
saved, they will come to you and say: "Can we start a
group to bring our unsaved friends to where they can
hear the gospel?" Then you know that they are ready
to work in partnership with you. Then you know that
you are ready to build "fruit that will last".*

Fruit That Will Last *page 148*

Task 2: Feed your sheep

Once you have **found** your sheep, the second task of a New
Testament shepherd is to **feed** your sheep. If you think
about an actual shepherd with actual sheep (the woolly
variety!), then you will see that this makes sense. No use
going out, risking your life, and gathering your sheep
together to have them all starve to death! The shepherd
needs to guide his sheep to green pastures; he needs to
take them to clear waters.

The well-known words from Psalm 23 bear this out.

The LORD is my shepherd, I shall not be in want. He makes me lie down in green pastures, he leads me beside quiet waters. **Psalm 23:1-2**

Good shepherds feed their sheep!

a) The example of Jesus

If you were Jesus, and you saw that the very people that you were trying to reach were like sheep without a shepherd, and you wanted to start feeding them—how would you do it?

When Jesus landed and saw a large crowd, he had compassion on them, because they were like sheep without a shepherd. So he began teaching them many things. **Mark 6:34**

"He began teaching them many things." That's how he fed them. That's how he shepherded them. That's how Jesus prepares his disciples for ministry. **He feeds them by teaching them God's word.**

There is an amazing verse near the end of Luke's Gospel. Jesus has risen from the dead, but his disciples are confused. They don't know what's happened. Their leader has been killed—and now his tomb is empty. The risen Jesus comes alongside them, but they do not recognise him; and a conversation takes place.

Jesus' disciples need to be fed. They are at a very weak and vulnerable point. Their faith is about to be snuffed out, and they need to be strengthened. Jesus, the master shepherd, is about to feed them. Listen in to Luke's recollection of this:

> *And beginning with Moses and all the Prophets,*
> *[Jesus] explained to them what was said in all the*
> *Scriptures concerning himself.*   **Luke 24:27**

Can you imagine being there? Having Jesus himself conduct a Bible study and show you everything you need to know all the way from Moses and the prophets? That's what Jesus did to feed his sheep. He taught them God's word.

If you're going to be a faithful shepherd, you need to faithfully teach God's word. Jesus himself sets us this example.

b) The command of Jesus

There is a fascinating encounter between Jesus and Peter which occurs after Jesus has been raised from the dead. Before Jesus had died, Peter had denied him three times. This is their first personal encounter since then, and three times Jesus shows Peter that he has totally restored their relationship. In so doing he commissions Peter for his ongoing ministry.

Three times Jesus asks Peter whether he loves him, and three times Peter replies that he does. On each of these three occasions, there is a command from Jesus to Peter. A challenge that will guide his ongoing ministry.

You can check out this encounter in John 21:15-17:

> *Feed my lambs.*   **John 21:15**
>
> *Take care of my sheep.*   **John 21:16**
>
> *Feed my sheep.*   **John 21:17**

If you want to be a faithful shepherd… if you want to be a faithful youth leader… you need to be careful to "feed your sheep".

c) How the body grows

God has given us a plan so that the whole body of Christ grows. A plan to ensure that Christian congregations grow in a healthy way. A plan to ensure that youth groups grow strong in a way that bears much fruit.

Although the New Testament speaks often about "shepherds", most modern translations only use the word "pastor" once. But this one usage of the word "pastor" shows us how we are to feed our sheep.

> *It was he who gave some to be apostles, some to be*
> *prophets, some to be evangelists, and some to be*
> *pastors and teachers, to prepare God's people for*
> *works of service, so that the body of Christ may be*
> *built up.*   ***Ephesians 4:11-12***

What is God's plan to feed and grow his sheep? The passage goes on to talk about how every Christian is given spiritual gifts by God—which are to be used to minister to others—and that when every Christian is carrying out their ministry, then the whole body will grow.

But where does it start?

It starts with "apostles, prophets, evangelists, pastors and teachers". What is the common thread in all these spiritual gifts from God? **They all centre around proclaiming and teaching God's word.**

Apostles take God's word to plant and start new ministries.

Prophets take God's word and apply it to the life of an individual.

Evangelists take God's word and call people to follow Jesus.

Pastors and teachers take God's word to teach and grow believers in their faith.

That's how God's people grow! **That's** how God's sheep are fed. Pastors (shepherds) teach them God's word!

And what's the point?

> *To prepare God's people for works of service, so that the body of Christ may be built up.* ***Ephesians 4:12***

When God's word is taught faithfully, it "prepares God's people for works of service". That is, good Bible teaching helps activate Christians into ministry. That's the way Christians are fed so that they grow. And when **that** happens, the whole body of Christ is built up.

The second task of a shepherd is to "feed his sheep" by taking God's word and applying it to their lives.

d) The key task of a youth leader

The key task of a youth leader is to be able to teach God's word. Some will stand in front of thousands and preach their hearts out. Some will lead small groups and apply God's word to each individual's life. Some will teach God's word "one on one" by taking biblical principles and communicating them by serving. All sorts of spiritual gifts are needed across the spectrum of youth leaders. But our central task remains the same as it was for Jesus himself— to feed our sheep by teaching them God's word.

How do I do that?

You don't need a degree from a theological college. You don't need to be a street-corner preacher. You might have to do some work, you might have to do some study, you might have to learn how to teach God's word in a better way. But anyone can start, because God has placed some sheep in our care and they already need feeding.

Here are three key steps to help grow you as a faithful shepherd who feeds their sheep:

i. Find out what God's word really means
Don't just take a passage and make it mean anything you want it to say. Try and find out what God really meant when he first caused this to be written down. There are plenty of books and resources that can help you with this. Plenty of courses you can attend. Plenty of Christian leaders you can ask for help. You will find that the more you study the Bible, the more you are able to work out what God's original message first meant.

More about this in Chapter 14!

ii. Apply God's word to your own life first
If you want to be an effective communicator of God's word, then you need to make sure it is working in your own life first. You can't expect to get others to live by God's word if you're not living by it yourself! God's word living in your life will communicate far more powerfully than anything you say!

iii. Help others to apply it to their life
Once you've got God's word working in your own life, see if you can help others to apply it to themselves. As a faithful shepherd, you need to know your sheep and understand your sheep (that third important relationship!), and help them work out what needs to change so that God's word will be living and active in their life.

e) But I'm not a "Bible teacher"!

Every one of us has different spiritual gifts. Not all of us are teachers. And yet all shepherds need to make sure that the sheep are fed—with good teaching. That's fine if you already feel that you are a solid preacher, or an effective small-group leader. But what if you're thinking: *"I don't think I can do this. I know my sheep need good teaching, but I'm not sure I can do it."*

Two suggestions:

i. Use other great teachers

There are plenty of effective Bible teachers—and you can listen to them and learn from them on podcasts, DVD etc. Some of the world's best preachers are available to your youth group so that your sheep are fed. Remember, the shepherd's job is to make sure that the sheep are fed. **You don't have to do all the feeding!**

You probably know some good Bible teachers from your own church—or from other churches, who can come and help out. Don't be scared to ask.

And by listening to other good Bible teachers, you will probably become a better Bible teacher yourself!

ii. Pray that God raises up good teachers

You do not have, because you do not ask God.

James 4:2

If you want your youth group to have good Bible teachers, **pray that God raises up good Bible teachers**. This is a prayer that he will love to answer. There may be other people in your congregation—or other leaders in your youth ministry—whom God will raise up to teach his word. God has limitless resources. He could cause someone new to come to your church who has a heart for teaching God's word to young people. If there is a spiritual gift that is needed in your ministry, **ask God to raise someone up with that gift!**

Be prepared for God to use YOU.

If God has placed you as a shepherd over his sheep, he might just want you to be the person whom he equips to teach his word to his people. God can give spiritual gifts whenever he wants and to whomever he wants. Are you prepared to be the one whom he enables to teach? Are you willing to give it a go? Start with smaller groups—and ask for feedback. People will usually tell you whether you are being used powerfully by God or not.

Many years ago I visited a large youth ministry in the United States. They had a big programme which attracted thousands. Central to their ministry was having their youth pastor stand before this crowd and preach God's word. And he was good! Powerfully good! I could see how God was using him effectively, and how his excellent preaching was central to the whole process.

He was encouraging me to think through our own ministry— to turn it from an "entertainment–based" youth group to a "proclaiming God's gospel" youth group. (See the full story in *Fruit That Will Last*.) I said to him: *"But I can't preach like that"*. I couldn't see how his style of programme could work unless there was a central, effective Bible teacher.

His suggestion? *"Ask God to develop you as a preacher. Try it. Trust him."* I did. I started small, and built strong. And God enabled me to communicate his word effectively, and preaching soon became a feature of our youth ministry. I am now in the privileged position of being able to raise up many others in my leadership team to also be effective preachers of God's word.

For some helpful resources on how to understand and teach God's word, please refer to the recommendations in Appendix 3 (page 303).

Task 3: Fight for your sheep
You want to be a faithful shepherd?

Only three things to do:

You find your sheep.

You feed your sheep.

You fight for your sheep.

Fighting for your sheep—guarding your sheep—really matters. If you think about an actual shepherd with actual sheep (the woolly variety!), then you will see that this makes sense. You have put your life on the line by finding them. You have worked hard to guide them to green pasture and clear water so that they can be fed—and to continue to grow strong and healthy. Now you need to guard them—so that they don't wander away, and so that wolves do not come in and devour them.

a) Guard them against going astray
Have a look at this great picture of God—the perfect shepherd—gathering up those who have strayed.

> *For this is what the Sovereign LORD says: I myself will search for my sheep and look after them. As a shepherd looks after his scattered flock when he is with them, so will I look after my sheep. I will rescue them from all the places where they were scattered*

*on a day of clouds and darkness. I will bring them
out from the nations and gather them from the
countries, and I will bring them into their own land.
I will pasture them on the mountains of Israel, in
the ravines and in all the settlements in the land. I
will tend them in a good pasture, and the mountain
heights of Israel will be their grazing land. There they
will lie down in good grazing land, and there they
will feed in a rich pasture on the mountains of Israel.
I myself will tend my sheep and make them lie down,
declares the Sovereign LORD. I will search for the lost
and bring back the strays.* **Ezekiel 34:11-16**

One of the real problems of being a youth leader is having
sheep who go astray. Teenagers can sometimes be so full-
on for Jesus one minute, and then be in deep, unrepentant
sin the next. There are so many attractions and distractions
to entice a young person to walk away from Jesus. A real
part of being a faithful shepherd is to guard your sheep
against going astray.

Sometimes that means taking the extra time to care for
a young person who is being less than co-operative.
Sometimes it means the phone call at midnight and
disrupted sleep. Sometimes it means driving to far-flung
places to rescue a teenager who has got themselves into a
mess. Sometimes it simply means making the phone call to
say: *"I haven't seen you at church for the last few weeks—is
everything okay?"*

The faithful shepherd doesn't let sheep just wander away
without taking action to rescue them and bring them back.
In Ezekiel 34:16, God says: *"I will search for the lost and
bring back the strays"*. That describes the heart of God, the
perfect shepherd. Does that describe your heart as well?

b) Guard them against wolves

When Paul was leaving his instructions to the leaders at the church in Ephesus, he warned them to be good shepherds so they could guard against the wolves who would ravage the flock of God.

> *Keep watch over yourselves and all the flock of which the Holy Spirit has made you overseers. Be shepherds of the church of God, which he bought with his own blood. I know that after I leave, savage wolves will come in among you and will not spare the flock. Even from your own number men will arise and distort the truth in order to draw away disciples after them. So be on your guard!*   **Acts 20:28-31**

These "wolves" who will come in and savage the flock are not mainly bad people from the outside. They are people **from within the church** who will seek to lead young sheep away from the true path that Jesus has laid out for them. As a shepherd, you need to guard your young flock from "wolves".

How? By strong Bible teaching so that they:

> *will no longer be infants, tossed back and forth by the waves, and blown here and there by every wind of teaching and by the cunning and craftiness of men in their deceitful scheming.*   **Ephesians 4:14**

You equip your sheep to be strong by applying good Bible teaching to their lives so that they will not be led astray by false teaching. Sometimes this will mean standing up to those who would lead them astray.

Some years ago, I was working with a young man in his senior year at high school. He had only recently become a

Christian, and he was in a small Bible-study group with me, slowly growing in his faith.

One day he said to me: "I'm going to another Bible-study group as well".

When I made a few enquiries, I worked out that he was attending a Mormon Bible study. Now, many Mormons are fantastic people, but they have a faith and a belief that is **way different** from what the Bible teaches. As he was a very young Christian, I knew that he was not yet strong enough or wise enough to know the difference between good Bible teaching, and false Bible teaching. So on subsequent occasions when we met, I told him that he should stop attending the Mormon Bible study, and I tried to give him some warning about their false beliefs. In the end, he trusted me, and he stopped attending. I had done my job as a shepherd—I had guarded my sheep, and I thought the story was finished.

The next week, there was a lady waiting for me at my doorstep when I arrived home. She was the Mormon Bible teacher. She wanted to confront me; she was not a happy person at all. She was fairly wound up.

"How dare you vilify Mormons! How dare you slander us! How dare you try to influence young minds to be prejudiced against us!" She wanted to invoke the Australian Racial Vilification Act against me. She wanted to stop me having access to the local state high school. She wanted me to publicly retract any negative comment I had made about the Mormons. She was going to the authorities. She wanted my blood. And, can I add, she was a very scary lady.

Nervously, I asked her some questions. *"Can I check with you that I understand what you believe and teach?"* I then proceeded to ask her a series of questions about Mormon belief (and for simplicity, her answer was *"Yes"* to each one of these).

"Our God whom we worship, is he just one of thousands of other gods?"

"These thousands of other Gods—is each one of them god over another galaxy just like our God is god over this galaxy?"

"Did our God have parents and grandparents?"

"Did our God start life as a man?"

"Did our God have sex with his wife, and conceive us as spirit children, so we could then be born on earth so that this galaxy would be populated?"

"If I follow the Mormon teachings, and marry a girl who follows the Mormon teachings, and we get married in a Mormon temple, then when we die, will we become God and Mrs God of a distant galaxy, just like our God (and Mrs God) are god over this galaxy?"

"As God and Mrs God, will my wife and I have eternal sex, to conceive spirit children, so that we populate a distant galaxy, just like God and Mrs God did in this galaxy?"

I then looked at her—square in the eyes—and I said: *"Lady—the god you believe in is **nothing like** the God that the Bible talks about. I will not allow you to lead astray young Christians who don't know any better. You are a wolf in sheep's clothing and I will do anything it takes to protect the sheep that God has given into my care."*

She left. She returned to Utah for further study. I recovered from my encounter. But sometimes that's what it takes to be a faithful shepherd! You must fight for your sheep—you must guard your sheep from the wolves that will devour.

In this case, the false teaching was obvious – but remember, the "wolves" Paul was talking about were people **from within the church**. Threats to your young flock can be much more subtle than that Mormon teacher. To protect your sheep, you need to keep your eyes open. That's not to say anyone and everyone in your church is a threat! But if you're concerned about something that someone else within the church is teaching the young people, don't ignore it. Ask yourself: *"If the young people believe what they are saying, will it mean they stop knowing Jesus as both their Lord and their Saviour? Will it mean they no longer treat the Bible as God's word?"* If the answer is "Yes", you need to **defend your flock**.

c) Guard them against thieves

In Jesus' day, shepherds had to take their job very seriously. The shepherd only had a small number of sheep. Every single one was precious to him. He could not afford to lose one at all. He would guard them—even at the risk of his own life.

At night, there was usually no secure building where the sheep would be safe from the ravaging wolves. The shepherd would often herd the sheep into a natural corner, where maybe a hedge and a fence formed a horseshoe formation—a small circle with only one entrance. The shepherd would gather his sheep in this small corner, settle them down for the night, and then, to ensure their safety, the shepherd himself would sleep across the entrance to this makeshift sheep-fold.

The shepherd became the gateway or the door to the sheep. No one could come in or out without disturbing the shepherd. No thief could enter and make off with a month's supply of roast lamb! And more importantly, the shepherd was able to guard his sheep against the hungry wolves by laying his own body in the way of danger.

> *Therefore Jesus said again, "I tell you the truth, I am the gate for the sheep. All who ever came before me were thieves and robbers, but the sheep did not listen to them. I am the gate; whoever enters through me will be saved. He will come in and go out, and find pasture. The thief comes only to steal and kill and destroy; I have come that they may have life, and have it to the full."* **John 10:7-10**

There will be those who are only in ministry for what they can get out of it themselves. There will be leaders who will use their sheep for their own advantage. The cause of Jesus is dragged through the mud every time a minister or youth leader is discovered being dishonest, or involved in sexual sin. The thief only comes to steal and kill and destroy. The youth leader who is a true shepherd comes to give the life that Jesus offers. I would do anything it takes to guard one of my young people against another leader who was only a thief.

d) Guard them with your own life

> *I am the good shepherd. The good shepherd lays down his life for the sheep. The hired hand is not the shepherd who owns the sheep. So when he sees the wolf coming, he abandons the sheep and runs away. Then the wolf attacks the flock and scatters it. The*

> *man runs away because he is a hired hand and cares*
> *nothing for the sheep.* **John 10:11-13**

There are two sorts of leaders pictured here. One is called the "hired hand". This is the person who is just doing their job. Maybe they're a youth leader because the minister asked them. Maybe there was nobody else. But they do their job—they mind the sheep—and everything looks okay.

The other leader is the true shepherd. This person cares deeply for his sheep. This leader would do anything to ensure their survival and growth.

Both leaders look the same for a while. Both are looking after their sheep. How do you tell the difference? What is the key that makes one a good shepherd, and one only a hired hand?

Jesus explains that the essential difference is displayed **when it gets hard**. When the wolves come. When the shepherd has to make a decision as to whether he will protect his own life, or protect his sheep. The hired hand runs away screaming: *"No one ever told me it would be this hard! I'm out of here!"* The good shepherd lays down his life for his sheep. That is the difference.

Jesus paid the ultimate price for being a good shepherd. When he was strung up on that cross, he gave up his life, so that we *"may have life, and have it to the full"* (John 10:10).

So... what sort of a youth leader are you? A faithful shepherd... or a hired hand? How do you handle it when things get tough in your leadership? How do you react when it's rough going and you're not seeing many results? How do you deal with it when group members disappoint you and let you down? How do you survive when outside influences entice your young people away from the path that you know they should travel? How do you react to the young person who is having a terrible time, and needs someone to hang in with them as they travel in very murky territory? Will you hang in there with the teenager who is fighting against you and treating you horribly as you attempt to care for them?

The hired hand runs away. The good shepherd gives up his life for his sheep.

Which is it for you?

Chapter 6
You are a servant

1. Who's really important?

a) In our world

We live in a crazy world. There are some people whom we place on a pedestal—worshipping and honouring them with an almost god-like status. There are others whom we more or less ignore, and who rarely get any recognition from us. But here's the crazy bit! Sometimes the most **valuable** people are the most ignored!

Who do we turn into heroes? Who gets god-like recognition wherever they go? Who gets paid mega-bucks and lives a life of fame and glory?

Usually a rock star—or a movie star—or a sports star!

And good luck to them! But sometimes if you check out their lifestyle—when you look at the way they live, when you see what their moral standards are, you might think these are the absolutely **worst** idols to have as role models for our young people. Some of them jump in and out of bed with assorted partners from within the human and animal kingdom; some of them use language which focuses your attention on all the vilest acts of degradation; some of them treat others in a way which suggests they're just objects to be used.

Do you get my drift? They are good at their chosen profession (music, sport, whatever), and we turn them into idols, whether they deserve it or not.

On the other hand, there is a different group of people in our world who are **extremely** valuable in what they do—and yet rarely ever get noticed, and are often under-paid and under-appreciated. Nurses are a good example. Where would we be without them? Yet apart from Florence Nightingale, none of them ever gets a mention. Absolutely vital to our health and well-being. Often sacrificial in their tasks. If you've ever been in hospital, you know the great work they do. Usually underpaid. Often unappreciated. No glamour lifestyle. No mega-bucks. No celebrity status. Yet **incredibly** valuable.

It's a crazy world we live in—where some people are exalted and others are ignored.

b) Leaders

How we think about leaders can vary between these two extremes. In some cultures, leaders are exalted and revered. They carve huge likenesses of their leaders into the sides of mountains. Successful leaders are honoured. They are addressed with respectful titles. They are powerful and influential. A cut above the rest of humanity.

At the other extreme, there is the cynical attitude that many of us show. We make fun of our leaders. We pull them down at every opportunity. We love to see them fail. We resent it when they tell us what to do. The thought that we would ever carve huge likenesses of our leaders into the side of a mountain is ludicrous! *"Who do they think they are? They're no better than anyone else!"*

Yet even in our sceptical western culture, there is real status in being a leader. The CEO of a large multi-national company will have a million-dollar-plus salary. The managing director of a firm will have a huge office with plush leather chairs. The chairman of the board will have the key to the executive washroom. School principals will have their own reserved parking space. Mayors have fancy chains they wear around their necks. Even senior pastors have bigger desks than their youth pastors do!

c) Youth leaders

There can be real status in being a youth leader. I remember when I was at Bible college. I went to an institution that is very well respected in my church circles. When I met church people, and they asked me, *"What do you do?"*, I had a real confidence in saying proudly: *"I'm a student at Moore College"*. *"Really!"* they would reply, with terms of respect and envy. It felt good. I was on the way up.

I was at a church once where the real mark of success was to be invited to be a youth leader. Being asked on to the team was seen as the stamp of approval from Jesus himself. Christians who didn't get invited to be a youth leader... well... they were sort of treated like they came from a spiritual "reject shop".

Teenagers will sometimes give you instant status when you become a youth leader. They suddenly have an ally who is "a bit older", or "a bit taller", or "a bit more confident", or "a bit richer". They have a friend who is "so much cooler than my parents". They will look up to you, listen to you, imitate you, and model themselves on you.

Instant status. Instant recognition. Buried deep within our psyches is the notion that "leaders really are more important".

2. The servant-leader

Jesus turns our normal ideas about leadership upside down. He shifts our thinking from perceiving that a leader is someone great, to showing us that the true leader is a genuine servant.

a) The privilege of being last

It was embarrassing, really. Jesus' disciples had been arguing about who was the greatest. About who should have the place of honour. About who was the best leader. About who was the most important. Jesus knew what was in their hearts and he questioned them about it.

They came to Capernaum. When he was in the house, he asked them, "What were you arguing about on the road?" But they kept quiet because on the way they had argued about who was the greatest.

Mark 9:33-34

How embarrassing! Here you are having a quiet party-room leadership brawl, and Jesus catches you out! Ouch!

Jesus has something very important to teach his disciples about leadership. Listen in.

Sitting down, Jesus called the Twelve and said, "If anyone wants to be first, he must be the very last, and the servant of all." He took a little child and had him stand among them. Taking him in his arms, he said to them, "Whoever welcomes one of these little children

> *in my name welcomes me; and whoever welcomes*
> *me does not welcome me but the one who sent me."*
> **Mark 9:35-37**

In the culture of Jesus' time, children were the bottom of the pile. They had no rights, and were often discarded by their society. No self-respecting leader would ever spend time with them.

And yet Jesus shows his followers the heart of being a servant-leader. *"If anyone wants to be first, he must be the very last, and the servant of all."*

Jesus is teaching us something powerful about being a leader in his kingdom. If you want to be first—if you want to be great—fantastic! Here's how you do it. You put yourself—and your interests—and your status last. That's what a servant does.

Very few youth leaders ever want to hear this. Many of us want to be leaders because we want to be looked up to. Jesus is saying: *"Are you prepared to put yourself **last**?"*

b) The privilege of being a servant

Have you ever wanted to be the leader who is picked for the best job? Perhaps you're in a team of leaders, and they're looking for someone to be in charge next year. Or the senior pastor is looking for someone to accompany him in his Lear Jet to an overseas conference. Or perhaps you want to make sure that you get to be the up-front speaker more often. Or they're trying to decide which leader gets the only en-suite room at the campsite. Or who gets the double bed. Or seconds of ice cream.

Jesus' disciples were fighting over who would get the best job. Who would Jesus pick to sit at his right hand and his left hand—in the places of honour—when he came back to rule the universe in glory? James and John thought they were star material. And they knew how to network!

"Hey—let's go and ask Jesus for the best positions in leadership! Let's get in before any of the other disciples do!"

Listen in again!

Then James and John, the sons of Zebedee, came to him. "Teacher," they said, "we want you to do for us whatever we ask." "What do you want me to do for you?" he asked. They replied, "Let one of us sit at your right and the other at your left in your glory."
                                                                                    Mark 10:35-37

Jesus deals with their request. He points out that they don't know what they're asking for. He tells them that he's not interested in playing their petty power games. But the other disciples get wind of what's going on, and they get aggro with James and John for trying to get into Jesus' good books. *(Check this out in Mark 10:38-41.)*

Jesus then goes on to give us some of the most revolutionary teaching about being a leader. He is presenting his model for those who will lead in his name. He is giving the blueprint for anyone who wants to be a pastor, an elder or a youth leader.

i. Don't throw your weight around

Jesus called them together and said, "You know that those who are regarded as rulers of the Gentiles lord it over them, and their high officials exercise authority over them."
                                                                                    Mark 10:42

Jesus is saying: *"If you become a leader, then don't throw your weight around. Don't let power go to your head. Don't pull rank on others like the pagans do. I'm not calling you to be a leader so you can get a fancy badge and a long title. You're not there as a leader to show everyone how great you are."*

ii. Lead as a servant

Not so with you. Instead, whoever wants to become great among you must be your servant, and whoever wants to be first must be slave of all. **Mark 10:43-44**

Jesus is saying: *"Do you want to be great? Fantastic! Then learn how to be a servant. Do you want to be first? Marvellous! Then learn how to be a slave."*

This is not an easy lesson to learn!

In my early leadership days, I was feeling pretty special being a cabin leader on a week-long camp. Kids had come from all over the place, and I was in charge of a whole cabin group. I felt kind of important.

It rained all week! We were desperate to get some activities done. I managed to negotiate a deal with the cooks that my group would be allowed into the kitchen to cook some chips (that's "French fries" for my American friends!). That night, nine junior-high boys and I made the greasiest, most fat-laden chips ever imagined. And after our culinary success, we sat down and pigged ourselves out on our high-cholesterol delicacy.

Late that night—long after we were all asleep—our fat-laden gluttony started to take its toll. Tom was sleeping in the bunk above me. In the wee small hours of the morning, his stomach started its own internal revolution. Everything he had eaten that night—along with a month's supply of digested carrots—were all expelled from his writhing contorted body.

Tom was a smart kid. Even though he did not have time to get out of bed and run to the bathroom, he was quick-thinking enough not to vomit in his own bed. So he carefully leant over the side of his top bunk, and vomited on the floor.

What he was unaware of was that I had left my suitcase on the floor with the lid open. In the darkness of the night, he emptied the entire contents of his 14-year-old body into that very suitcase, and it overflowed onto the floor!

I was jolted awake by this internal explosion. I helped Tom clean himself up; changed his bedding; put his soiled sleeping bag out to wash in the morning; and lent him my sleeping bag. He was tired, and went back to sleep. No one else in the room stirred—and I was left cleaning the vomit from the floor and from out of my bag for hours and hours through the night.

God had given me a very quick lesson in servant leadership!

> *Not so with you. Instead, whoever wants to become great among you must be your servant, and whoever wants to be first must be slave of all.* **Mark 10:43-44**

If we had a world-wide army of Christian youth leaders who had developed servant hearts—and whose genuine goal was to humble themselves so that others would be pointed to Christ…

If we had teams of Christian youth leaders who were not focused on fulfilling their own agendas, or satisfying their own need for fulfilment, or promoting themselves to attain greatness and recognition...

If we could inspire a whole generation to truly take on the heart of Jesus and become "servant-leaders"...

then who knows the impact that we could make on this world for Jesus?

And here's the exciting news! **You have the opportunity to be part of that new generation of servant-leaders!**

iii. Jesus shows us how

Jesus did not come as some grand dictator who issued edicts saying: *"You must be my servants"*. When he calls us to servant-leadership, he is merely calling upon us to follow the very example he himself has set. Do you want to know what it means to lead as a servant? Then look no further than Jesus.

> *"For even the Son of Man did not come to be served, but to serve, and to give his life as a ransom for many."*　　　　　　　　　　　　　**Mark 10:45**

If ever there was a leader who had the right to be served, it was Jesus. If ever there was a leader who could simply demand that we should give up our life for him, it was Jesus. But it was he himself who served us first. It was he himself who gave up his life for us.

You want to be a great youth leader? It's simple.

Have the same heart that Jesus had.

Lead the same way Jesus did.

Learn to be a servant-leader.

3. The servant heart of Jesus

What's one of the hardest things about raising up a leadership team? What's one of the key issues in growing a leader who really will achieve what Jesus wants?

Attitude. Sometimes we are attracted by a leader's gifts or dazzling abilities, but what you're really after is the right attitude. The superstar leader who can do everything by themselves but has an attitude that puts down everyone else, and who never co-operates with the rest of the team... well... that's an attitude you can do without!

What sort of attitude do you want in every single youth leader?

a) Have the same attitude as Jesus

Your attitude should be the same as that of Christ Jesus.   ***Philippians 2:5***

If you want to be a great youth leader, then you need to model yourself on Jesus. You need to train your mind so that you will think like he does. You will need to train your reactions so you will react like he does. You will need to change your behaviour so you act like he does. You will need to change your leadership so you lead like he does. You will need to change your attitude to have the same attitude that he has.

And what sort of attitude does Jesus have?

b) Jesus did not claim his own rights

Who, being in very nature God, did not consider equality with God something to be grasped.
Philippians 2:6

Jesus is the Son of God. Always has been. Always will be. He came to earth with all the power and authority that belongs to God and God alone. That might and magnificence was there for him to claim. He had every right to it. He deserved it.

And yet he was born to a peasant woman in a cultural backwater of the Roman Empire. He was born into land that was occupied by a foreign power. He was born as a Jew—a culture despised by their Roman overlords. He lived in poverty. He lived in an era when life was very brutal and very harsh. He trod the same roads as the down-and-outs and shared our frustrations as an oppressed citizen of planet earth. He was wrongfully arrested, unfairly tried, cruelly convicted, brutally tortured, and shamefully executed.

Even when he was hanging on the cross, his tormentors taunted him by crying out: *"Come down from the cross and save yourself"* (Mark 15:30). And he could have. At any moment he could have claimed his rights to the might and power of being God himself. He could have claimed his rights—and saved himself.

Yet he *"did not consider equality with God something to be grasped."* He did not claim his own rights and save himself. He gave up his rights to save you.

You probably have many rights as a youth leader. You might have the right to be respected. You might have the right to be listened to. You might have the right to have the most comfortable bed. You might have the right to extra servings of dessert at camp. You have the right to an attorney. You have the right to remain silent. You have a right to say what you are thinking. You might even have the right to demand others' attention and loyalty.

If you are going to have a servant heart—and have the same attitude as Jesus—then you will be a leader who is prepared to give up your rights. To stop pursuing your personal agenda. To be determined that you will lead the same way that Jesus does. To be committed to lead with a servant heart.

c) Jesus humbled himself as a servant

But [he] made himself nothing, taking the very nature of a servant, being made in human likeness. And being found in appearance as a man, he humbled himself and became obedient to death—even death on a cross!   ***Philippians 2:7-8***

Jesus' decision to be a servant was not an academic exercise. He was not studying "Servanthood 101" to obtain a college diploma. He was not entering into a televised debate on the topic and trying to sway a crowd so they would vote him as the cleverest and funniest in his arguments. His servant leadership led him to the humiliation of death on a cross.

This is the sort of leadership that this world needs. This is the sort of leadership that God's church needs. This is the sort of leadership which the students in your youth group need. This is the sort of leader—this is the sort of servant—that God is calling you to be.

What does it mean to be a servant-leader?

Chapter 7 awaits you!

Chapter 7
Ten marks of a servant-leader

What does it really mean to be a servant-leader? The New Testament has much to say about the role of a servant. Here are ten key marks of a biblical servant.

1. You know how to take orders

We don't really live in a world where we use terms like "servant and master". Perhaps we more readily understand terms like "employee and boss", or maybe "student and teacher". But do you get the relationship? The essence of being a servant is that you have a master; you recognise the authority of your master; and you serve your master.

The servant leader always recognises that they are a **servant** before they are a leader. God is the master who gives us the privilege of serving in his household. And the key to being a good servant is that you know how to take orders from your master!

Jesus encounters a centurion—an army officer who had command over 100 other soldiers. His daughter is very sick, and he recognises the authority that Jesus has to give a command and heal her. He explains to Jesus **why** he knows that Jesus has that authority:

> *For I myself am a man under authority, with soldiers under me. I tell this one, "Go," and he goes; and that one, "Come," and he comes. I say to my servant, "Do this," and he does it.*   ***Matthew 8:9***

That is the role of a servant. The master says to his servant: *"Do this"*—and he does it. It's really that simple. God says: *"Do this"*—and the true servant does it. The true servant doesn't argue about it, or make excuses about it, or come back with a counter-proposal, or do it after checking their friends on *Facebook®*, or delay until the next ad break on the TV. The true servant knows how to take orders.

Just a quick check, now. Are you a true servant of God? When God tells you in his Bible *"Do this"*—do you do it? That is the mark of a servant. That is the mark of a servant leader.

This is an easy one to get back to front. We can actually end up thinking that **we** are the masters and that **Jesus** is our servant.

This can come through in our prayers. *"Dear Jesus, please make my tooth stop hurting. Dear Jesus, please give me a good mark in my exam. Dear Jesus, please get me a good job that will make me lots of money. Dear Jesus, please find me a girlfriend. Good boy, Jesus. Come here, Jesus. Go fetch, Jesus. Roll over, Jesus."*

Now, I know you would never pray that way. But sometimes God can be portrayed as, *"just your good buddy who sits down and has a cappuccino with you and wipes up the messes in your life"*. Yes—he certainly **does** serve us, but you need to understand your first relationship with him: he is the master and you are the servant!

> *A student is not above his teacher, nor a servant above his master.*　　　　　　　**Matthew 10:24**

> *I tell you the truth, no servant is greater than his master, nor is a messenger greater than the one who sent him.*　　　　　　　**John 13:16**

When your young people look at you, will they see you as a servant who readily takes orders from God, your master?

2. You are responsible for your tasks

It's like a man going away: He leaves his house and puts his servants in charge, each with his assigned task. **Mark 13:34**

Servants are given jobs to do. The master allocates them. That's how the household operates. Each servant is responsible to his master for fulfilling his duties. Each servant wants to please his master by doing his job well.

So too with God, our master. He has allocated tasks to you which he expects you to do well. He wants you to be faithful. He wants you to be reliable. He wants you to be responsible.

Some of these tasks come about by our relationships. What has God called you to be faithful in? Is he calling you to be a faithful mother or father—or perhaps to be a devoted son or daughter? Is he wanting you to be a reliable friend; a compassionate boss; a loyal employee; a hardworking sporting coach; or just a listening ear? The essence of being a servant is that you are responsible for the tasks that are assigned to you.

As a **servant-leader**, what are the tasks that God has allocated to you? Do you lead a small Bible-study group? Are you responsible for the overall youth group at your church? Is it your job to set out the chairs and help clean up afterwards? Do you make sure that the names and addresses are kept up to date? Are you on a prayer team? Do you follow up students who have made a commitment to Jesus?

The heart of being a servant-leader is that you are responsible for the tasks that are allocated to you. This is the sort of servant whom God is looking for to work in his household. This is the sort of servant who will perform valuable work in God's kingdom. This is the sort of servant who gives honour and glory to his master.

As a servant-leader, what tasks has God allocated to you? How are you going at being responsible for doing them well?

3. You are trusted with more when you are faithful

Guess what happens when you are faithful in the tasks that are allocated to you in ministry? **You get trusted with even more valuable things!**

Remember the master who had gone away and left his servants in charge with various responsibilities? When he returns, he checks up on one of his servants to see how he has gone with his allocated tasks:

> *His master replied, "Well done, good and faithful servant! You have been faithful with a few things; I will put you in charge of many things. Come and share your master's happiness!"*   **Matthew 25:21**

Did you catch the words that God will say to his servants who have proved themselves to be faithful? *"You have been faithful with a few things; I will put you in charge of many things."*

It can be so easy to think: *"My youth group's not worth much. We don't get many kids coming. If only we were like the church down the road. They've got **hundreds** of teens* *coming along! Boy, if I had that many students in my youth group, I know I'd really be doing well!"*

There's always a bigger and better ministry you are dreaming of. This is a good thing! It's great to plan to grow and to look for ways to improve your ministry to make it more effective. But when you start thinking that your current youth ministry isn't that valuable because it's so small—and you look longingly at what others are doing and try to imagine why God hasn't blessed you with success like that, and maybe you even move to a bigger church so you'll feel more important—then you've missed the heart of being a servant-leader.

A true servant **proves his faithfulness with the small responsibility he has been given**. Then, when the master sees that he is doing a good job, he will place him in charge of far bigger and more significant areas.

Do you want to be a leader in a youth ministry that reaches thousands of students?
Then be faithful with the dozen that God has given you already!

Do you want to be able to teach God's word in front of huge audiences?
Then be faithful in leading the Bible-study group of six students that God has given to you!

Do you want to have a $100,000 budget for your youth ministry?
Then be faithful with the $100 you already have responsibility for!

Do you want to be used by God to bring hundreds of young people to follow Jesus?

Then be faithful in following up the one teenager who is your responsibility now.

You don't have to promote yourself. You don't have to clamour for more recognition on the leadership ladder of success. You don't have to keep telling everyone what a great leader you are, hoping you'll be asked "for the really big stuff".

If you are faithful with a little, then you will be entrusted with much.

4. You are always ready to serve

Be dressed ready for service and keep your lamps burning, like men waiting for their master to return from a wedding banquet, so that when he comes and knocks they can immediately open the door for him. It will be good for those servants whose master finds them watching when he comes. I tell you the truth, he will dress himself to serve, will have them recline at the table and will come and wait on them. It will be good for those servants whose master finds them ready, even if he comes in the second or third watch of the night.   **Luke 12:35-38**

The true heart of a servant-leader is that they are always ready to serve. They don't have times where they're on duty and times where they can't be bothered. The true servant-leader is ready to serve at any time the master calls them.

My experience of youth ministry is that things rarely happen according to a neat timetable. Young people are not good at timing their crises to fit into your allocated leadership hours.

We always have "house-parents" at our camps. They're a set of parents who are there for the welfare of both leaders and students. I had invited a new couple to come on one of our camps for a week. *"You'll have a great time,"* I calmly informed them. *"Nothing ever goes wrong. You'll just hang around all week and develop great relationships with all the kids."*

It was the final night of camp. Everyone's emotions were a little raw. As we were heading off to bed, some of the kids were a little wound up. But we were all very tired. It had been a long week. All the leaders (especially this new set of house-parents) were very keen to hit the sack.

It was after lights-out that one of the female leaders came running to us: *"One of the students in my cabin is threatening to kill herself. I think she means it. What will I do?"*

We whirred into action. There was a girl to pacify and befriend; there were assorted students who were traumatised; there were leaders feeling very inadequate. A number of people in our team were called into action at this very late hour.

For our new house-parents, they got the privilege of accompanying this girl to the nearest hospital for a psychiatric assessment in the middle of the night! By the time they returned it was after 4am. They were on duty again at 7am. They were tired!

But they were servant-leaders. One of the marks of a servant-leader is that you are ready to serve at any time the master calls.

5. You follow Jesus

Whoever serves me must follow me; and where I am,
my servant also will be.   ***John 12:26***

If you are truly going to be a servant, you must follow Jesus.
You go where he goes. You do what he does. Wherever
Jesus is, that's where his servants will be as well.

You can't be a servant who just does what they feel like and
listens to Jesus as he passes by occasionally. You can't be
a servant by just having a belief system about Jesus. You
can't claim *"Jesus is my master"*, and then ignore the very
things he tells you to do. As Jesus says: *"Whoever serves me*
must follow me".

When it comes to servant-leaders—one of the marks of a
servant-leader is that they will follow Jesus. Now, this might
seem to be stating the obvious. *"Of course a Christian leader*
has to be a Christian! How could it ever be otherwise?"

I grew up in a Catholic family. I went to a Catholic school,
and the family all went to Catholic Mass. I never really
thought about following Jesus. I just did what the church
told me to do. I knew I was a good person. I didn't go
around breaking the commandments. I was a nice, sweet,
self-respecting, law-abiding Catholic boy. I believed it all,
but never thought about the idea of having a personal
relationship with Jesus.

When I left school, I was involved in coaching athletics. One
of my athletes invited me along to a rock concert being put
on by the youth group at his church. I went. It was a good
night. I enjoyed it. I thought it strange that rock musicians
would sing about Jesus (I mean, that's what priests talk
about in church, isn't it?). But the people were friendly, so I
went along to some other things that they ran.

I ended up in a Bible-study group; I went along to the camps; I got involved in running the youth group. I looked like a Christian. I sounded like a Christian. I **thought** I was a Christian. I sort of had some leadership qualities. I used to talk about "the other church I used to go to". I think people were impressed!

At the beginning of the next year, I was asked by the youth pastor if I would co-lead a small Bible-study group. Of course I said "yes". I mean, why not? That Easter we had a camp—but only for students in our Bible-study groups. It was only for Christians. I went along and joined in the fun.

The speaker that weekend kept asking people to start taking Jesus seriously, and commence a life of following him. I remember thinking that someone had given him the wrong guidelines. He was treating people like they needed to become Christians, when in fact everyone there was a Christian already! I thought I should mention this to him!

Before I had a chance, God spoke powerfully to me from his word. I wasn't a Christian! (Ouch!) I had Jesus as one of my hobbies—one of my interests—but I did not have him as my Lord and master. I was only playing at being a Christian. I wasn't really following Jesus at all.

So that weekend, very quietly, I gave my life to Jesus, and started on a journey of discovering more and more about him. I have never looked back since that day, and I praise God that he brought me to follow his Son before I could do too much damage to that Bible-study group as a **non-Christian leader**!

So it can happen. You can end up being a church youth leader without actually committing yourself to following Jesus.

Make sure that you—and all your fellow-leaders—don't miss out on one of the key marks of being a servant-leader. A true servant **follows Jesus**.

6. You serve the gospel

Have a listen to the apostle Paul:

> *I became a servant of this gospel by the gift of God's grace given me through the working of his power.*
> **Ephesians 3:7**

In many places Paul describes himself as a "servant of the gospel". The same is true of every servant-leader. You have been called to "serve the gospel".

The "gospel"—the great news about Jesus that changes lives—is all about the death and resurrection of Jesus. That's where the power is for lives to be changed as people believe this gospel, and trust their life to Jesus.

In everything that we do as leaders, we are called upon to serve that gospel. That is, our lives are meant to serve the purpose of helping people to see that Jesus' death and resurrection have changed us for ever. Similarly, the words we proclaim to others are meant to point them towards the saving power that is in Jesus as he dies and rises for them.

The true servant-leader will always be a servant of this gospel. That means that everything you do will promote the gospel of Jesus. And everything that you say will promote the gospel of Jesus. And this means that there is nothing that you will either say or do that will distract people from focusing on what Jesus has done for them.

This sounds pretty simple, but it is so easy to get it wrong.

In my early days as a youth pastor, the gospel was always "part" of what I did, but I do not think I was a true servant of that gospel. You see, much of what I did didn't point students to Jesus' death and resurrection. I think much of what I did actually pointed people to me and my terrific programmes.

I knew young people would hear about our group because we had fantastic outings. I knew they would come along because we had dynamic programmes. I knew they would learn to worship because we had an awesome band. I knew they would respond because I was delivering a powerful message.

Nothing wrong with these things in themselves. But I think we were really serving what **we** did, rather than what Jesus did. It is much more humbling to say: "*Lord, we will do our very best for you. But we know that you are the only one who can bring change to these students' lives. We will trust in the power of what your Son has done to bring miracles into the lives of our young people.*"

Paul says:

> *I am not ashamed of the gospel, because it is the power of God for the salvation of everyone who believes.*   **Romans 1:16**

God's gospel really works! Try it! Serve it! Do everything you can to point people to the saving work of Jesus for them on the cross!

This is what Paul says about leadership:

> *We always carry around in our body the death of Jesus, so that the life of Jesus may also be revealed in our body.*   **2 Corinthians 4:10**

Is that true of your ministry? The true servant-leader
always serves the gospel!

7. You flee from sin

Okay, it's confession time! When I scanned the New
Testament to find out everything it said about being a
servant, I wasn't expecting this one. I was expecting to
find verses on being humble, knowing my place, accepting
orders, serving others... you know—the traditional role of
a servant.

But these two verses kept staring at me. It was like God was
prodding me—to remind me of an essential quality of being
a faithful servant. A true servant, you see, **flees from sin**.

Let me share with you these two verses:

> *You, my brothers, were called to be free. But do not
> use your freedom to indulge the sinful nature; rather,
> serve one another in love.*   ***Galatians 5:13***

> *Live as free men, but do not use your freedom as a
> cover-up for evil; live as servants of God.*
>
> ***1 Peter 2:16***

Do you get the constant theme? In Galatians 5, serving
one another in love is the **opposite** of using your freedom
to indulge your sinful nature. In 1 Peter 2, living as God's
servant is the **opposite** of using your freedom as a cover-up
for evil.

It can be easy for a servant to confuse what "freedom" really
is. Freedom can be seen as "getting rid of every restraint",
"having no more rules", "having no more master telling me
what to do". Sometimes as Christians, we yearn for this sort
of freedom; we want to give up having to obey God's rules;

we want to be able to do "just as we please"; we kind of like the idea of escaping God's clutches so we don't have to do things his way any more.

So in Galatians 5, how can Paul urge us to be "free" by **serving** each other? The two sound like opposites!

It all gets down to understanding how God designed us. When God created us, he designed us with an **inbuilt dependency on him**. It's like designing a train—which is built to be totally dependent on its tracks. When the train stays on the railway line, it is free to achieve its potential as a train. As soon as a train goes "off the rails" (so to speak!), it is no longer free to be a train. If a train were to try and run along a road, or through a field, or up and down the beach, it would soon bog down, and would no longer have the freedom to achieve its potential as a train. The train's ability to be free is totally dependent on it staying on the rails that were designed for it.

So it is with us. God designed us with an inbuilt dependency on him. We were designed to run on his "rails". While we stick to God's way, we are free to reach our potential as humans. But when we want to break free from God's "rails"—and just do our own thing—we soon get bogged down in sin, and we are no longer free to achieve our God-given potential.

The true servant understands the freedom that they have in Christ, and doesn't keep breaking away from God's commands just so they can do their own thing. The true servant will run away from indulging their own sinful nature. The true servant will stay right away from evil.

Here are questions I need to ask myself as a servant-leader:

Do these statements above describe me as a true servant of God?

Do these statements above describe me as a servant-leader?

Is there anything I need to get rid of in my life so that I will be a more faithful servant of my heavenly master?

I encourage you to ask the same questions of yourself.

8. You accept persecution

For anyone wanting to be a servant of God, Jesus has some chilling words for you:

> *Remember the words I spoke to you: "No servant is greater than his master." If they persecuted me, they will persecute you also. If they obeyed my teaching, they will obey yours also. They will treat you this way because of my name, for they do not know the One who sent me.* **John 15:20-21**

Did you catch Jesus' words? *"If they persecuted me, they will persecute you also."* Ouch! These are hardly words that you would use to encourage people to sign up in a leadership-recruitment campaign!

But it makes sense. If a master is going to be persecuted by his enemies, then it follows that his servants will have a hard time too. Jesus was attacked—and eventually executed—by those who opposed him. It makes sense then that anyone who is his servant will be persecuted as well.

In many parts of our world, this persecution of Jesus' servants is still a life-or-death situation. But for many of us, it will take a more subtle form.

Servants will sometimes get taken for granted. If you put in "that extra effort", then some people will assume that you will *always* put in that much effort—and will demand it from you. You might not get thanked for your thoughtfulness. There might be no one who is appreciating you or encouraging you. Everyone else might leave all the jobs that they don't want to do—to you!

You might be ridiculed for your servant heart.

One year, in the football team I coach, one of the other dads became the assistant coach. I tried to genuinely care for each player, and did my best to serve each member of the team—including those who were of lower ability. He consistently ridiculed me for being "too soft-hearted". He said I had to be tougher on the boys. More demanding. More ruthless. Put the best eleven on every week. Stop babying the team-members so much.

It was hard to be a servant-leader in that situation. Being a servant was seen as "weakness" by my accuser. I often returned from training or match days feeling quite hurt and discouraged. And yet I tried to serve him as well (and I was somewhat vindicated when my team won the grand final!).

So **don't expect the world to love you** when you take on the role of a servant-leader. When you make yourself vulnerable to others, you'll sometimes get kicked in the stomach. When you genuinely try to serve others, you may find that they will use you as a doormat.

But remember the servant-leadership of your master:

> *For even the Son of Man did not come to be served,*
> *but to serve, and to give his life as a ransom for*
> *many.* **Mark 10:45**

It cost Jesus plenty to be a servant-leader. If you truly want to follow in his footsteps, it will cost you plenty as well.

9. You trust God's strength

If the previous point has made you a little reluctant to be a servant-leader, then let me encourage you…

God provides the gifts or abilities that you need to serve others.

God will provide the strength for you to continue to be a servant-leader.

Listen up!

> *Each one should use whatever gift he has received to*
> *serve others … If anyone serves, he should do it with*
> *the strength God provides, so that in all things God*
> *may be praised through Jesus Christ.* **1 Peter 4:10-11**

The only time you can "fail" at being a servant-leader is when you try to do it in your own strength. The only time you will "bomb out" as a servant-leader is when you're trusting in your own abilities.

It is a huge relief to know that it is God who gives us the abilities that we possess. Even the pagan world recognises this when they describe an unusually talented person as being "gifted". Here's the good news! **It doesn't all come from us!** We don't have to manufacture our own abilities or grow our own talents to be able to do what God has called us to do. If God has called you to a position of ministry or leadership, then he provides the gifts or abilities that you need to succeed in that! Yee-hah!

The same is true about providing the ongoing strength to persevere. Is leadership becoming a little exhausting? Do you no longer have the energy that you used to have? Do you sometimes feel that you're having absolutely no effect on anyone's life and you may as well chuck the whole thing in? (By the way—I feel all these on a regular basis!)

Perhaps it has been an unusually busy time for you. (The weeks leading up to running a camp are always like this for me!) It could be that there has been an unusual number of demands on your time by various people at different stages in their crises. Maybe you haven't been receiving much encouragement, and there is a gang of people at your church who keep criticising everything you do. Or it might just be that your time management ain't that good! There will always be times when you simply feel that you can't keep going.

Here is the danger. When you feel overloaded, you can drift into one of two inadequate solutions.

Number 1: Simply keep trying harder and harder and pushing yourself more and more.

Number 2: (this usually follows shortly after Number 1) Give up completely.

I have seen so many youth leaders go through this treadmill. Hard-working and visionary youth pastors who are feeling the crunch at their local church—and just keep pushing themselves harder and harder—until they finally give up, exhausted, disgruntled, and determined to never go down that track again.

I have caught myself on that same treadmill. It is not a pretty place to be!

There is an alternative. 1 Peter 4:11 says: *"If anyone serves, he should do it with the strength **God** provides"*. Here is my own editorial addition:

> *"And if you keep trying to do it in your own strength, you will wreck your health, you will wreck your faith, you will wreck your family, and you will wreck your ministry."*

God is there **just waiting to give you the strength you need to succeed as a servant-leader**. All you've got to do is ask! So when the going gets tough, the tough get praying! If life is becoming a bit of a whirlwind... if your ministry seems never-ending and frustrating... if there's never enough time in the day to get done what you want to get done—**then stop, and spend time with God, who will refresh you**.

God is not a master who wants to drive his servants into the ground with unreasonable demands on their time and energy. God is a master who wants to refresh you and uphold you so that you will achieve your very best—and enjoy it!

The heart of a servant-leader is to trust God for the strength that you need. Does that describe you?

10. You serve... wholeheartedly!

Do you know what the key mark of a servant is? Think about it—it is really so simple! Here is the key way to know if you have the heart of a servant.

A true servant... serves!

Would you like me to say that again? This is a point that has confused theologians throughout the ages. This is an aspect that has been missed by professors doing their PhD in "Servanthood". This can even be overlooked by rapidly-ageing youth pastors who write chapters about being a servant and overwhelm you by giving you ten separate points to think about!

Here it is—one more time.

A true servant... serves!

(Gasp! What deep truth!)

If you want to check out whether you are indeed a true servant-leader, then just ask yourself this question: *"Am I genuinely serving the people I lead?"* Because if you're not serving them, you'll only be serving yourself.

> *"Serve wholeheartedly, as if you were serving the Lord."*
> **Ephesians 6:7**

The Bible gives us two clues as to how to serve.

a) "Serve wholeheartedly..."

Or in other words—"with all your heart". No one wants a servant (or employee, or student, or worker, or helper, or volunteer, or youth leader) who only serves **reluctantly**. You don't want someone who will only **half-do** things. You don't want to be overseeing someone who **resents** everything they're doing.

"But you haven't seen some of the jobs I have to do!"

There will always be tasks that aren't exactly your favourite. Jobs that no one else really wants to do. Tasks that might be needed, but you find them a little bit tiresome. These are **fantastic** indicators of your servant heart! Anyone can work enthusiastically when they are doing a job that they really enjoy. But only a true servant can work wholeheartedly at something they're not actually enjoying!

So check it out! Can you work **wholeheartedly** at the parts of your ministry that you don't really enjoy? If you can—you are indeed developing the heart of a servant-leader.

b) "...as if you were serving the Lord"

This gives a whole new motivation for being a servant-leader. You do everything as if you were serving Jesus himself! You put out the chairs like you were putting them out for Jesus. You clean out the toilets like you were cleaning them for the Lord himself. You keep the paperwork accurate like you were keeping records for Jesus. You do your assignments like you were preparing them to present to Jesus.

Think about the ministry that you're involved in. Think about the leadership you exercise. As you think about the various aspects of it—the things you enjoy, as well as the things you find a little tiresome—can you honestly say that you do everything well and enthusiastically **like you were doing it for Jesus himself**? If so, congratulations—you are developing the heart of a servant-leader.

And if you're thinking to yourself: *"When those words were written in the Bible, they didn't understand the difficult situation I would be facing in my leadership! What do you mean: 'serve wholeheartedly—as if I were serving the Lord?'"*

Check back to those words in Ephesians 6. Look them up in your Bible. Who were these words being spoken to? They were being addressed to slaves who were held in captivity by their masters! That's right—the Bible was talking to people who were in the bondage of slavery, who might have had no hope of ever being set free, and many of whom served under wicked and cruel masters who abused them.

It's to those oppressed people that God says: *"Serve wholeheartedly, as if you were serving the Lord"*. So no matter what you are facing in your leadership, you too can be a true servant-leader—who will serve others wholeheartedly, and who will do it to the same standard of excellence as if you were serving Jesus himself.

Very simply, Jesus is a servant-leader. He gave up his life because of his love for those whom he served. If he has raised you up to be a leader, then he expects you to imitate him.

Every leader is always serving someone. You are either serving God, and the people he has given to you, or you are serving yourself.

Think carefully about your leadership. Which is it for you?

SECTION 2

Grow your leadership character

Chapter 8

You are developing your character

1. A lesson from the carpenter

What is it that makes one youth leader effective, and another not? If you want to be the best youth leader that you can possibly be, what is it that you need to work on? In God's view, what is the Number 1 area where he wants you to develop? What are the "tools of ministry" that you will carry with you that will make your Bible-teaching impactful, your message believable, your prayer passionate, and your pastoral relationships genuine?

Imagine this scene...

There's a carpenter getting ready for their day's work. In the morning, they don't just charge off to their first job and try to make something by shaping blocks of wood with their bare hands. Carpenters who try that sort of thing don't last long in the business of carpentry! Instead, a carpenter takes a set of tools to do their work—tools that they'll use to shape whatever pieces of wood they are working on. A carpenter without their tools is a carpenter who won't be effective at their work.

But it doesn't end here! If a carpenter has a full set of carpentry tools which are blunt, rusted, old or out of shape, then they will still be ineffective. Every tradesperson knows that it is not enough to simply have some tools with you! Those tools need to be in first-class condition for them to do a first-class job. Bad tools equals bad carpentry, regardless of how skilled the carpenter might be. If their tools are not up to the job, then even the world's best carpenter will not be able to produce a quality piece of work.

So what about the Christian leader who leaves for work— the work of helping people become more like Jesus? What are the tools that they will need to take with them?

Right now, we're not talking about things like the Bible. There are youth leaders all over the world who are teaching the Bible to people. Some are doing a great job of it—some are doing a lousy job. What's the essential difference? And we're not talking here about communication skills, or Bible-study research skills.

a) Your character is so important...
The main ministry tool that God has given you to develop... is your **character**!

If you knew that the person who was teaching you from the Bible was directly disobeying the very command that they are teaching—then what would you give them out of ten for their ministry? Probably about zero. It is the **character** of the leader that is the tool.

Just as the carpenter uses their saw to do their job, the Christian leader uses their own character to do their job. For the carpenter, the work is sawing the wood; and the tool is the saw. For the Christian leader, the work is teaching the Bible; and the tool is their character. For the carpenter, a blunt saw means a lousy job, no matter how hard they try. For the Christian leader, an un-Christlike character means lousy ministry, no matter how hard you try to teach the Bible.

Your character is your tool. Your whole life—the way that you live 24/7—is what you use to impact people for Jesus. Great character means the potential for great ministry. Lousy character means no fruitful ministry is possible, regardless of how skilled or gifted you are.

b) So keep it in top condition!

So what are the implications for Christian youth leaders? **You need to keep your character in top condition.** That is what Paul says to Timothy when he tells him these words:

Watch your life and doctrine closely. ***1 Timothy 4:16***

Your "doctrine" is what you teach; your "life" is the character that you use to teach it by example. This means that anything that you do to improve your own character— anything that you do that causes you to be more Christlike, anything that causes your own Christian life to grow—will automatically have a positive effect on those you are leading.

Imagine for a moment that you decide that you really have been treating your little sister a bit poorly and you feel convicted to change the situation. You then take the steps of apologising to her, making more of an effort to be genuinely interested in some of the things that she is doing, and being more polite.

Regardless of whether she responds favourably or not, a couple of things have just happened. You have repented of sin in your life, and your character has become more Christlike. A dull saw has just been sharpened. You have just repaired one of the tools that you need for ministry. What was in poor condition has been restored to enable you to be an effective leader.

Now that is well and good, but you might ask how that affects your ministry! The people you minister to have no idea who your sister is, let alone how well you treat her! What it means directly for your ministry is that you can now teach other people what God says about family relationships with **integrity**—because you are obeying what God says on this issue yourself.

In this sense, the Christian leader never has a minute off, let alone a day off. All the time, wherever you are, whatever you are doing, you are either leading by example in Christlike living, or else you are disobeying the very thing that you desperately want those whom you're leading to do. You want them to grow to be more and more like Jesus. Your life, your character, is your tool that will help make you either effective or ineffective in your ministry.

The carpenter's tools consist of what is in their toolbox. The Christian leader's tools consist of what is in their heart.

2. The character tree

Often in ministry the people who you are leading might not know what you are like when no one is looking. But God knows. He sees what you think, say and do all the time. He knows exactly how Christlike you are or are not. And God has set this world up so that you cannot have lasting success without the character to support it. Just like a tree has a trunk and branches above ground and then a root system below ground, a Christian leader has a ministry above ground (ie: people can see it) and they have their character below the ground (ie: not always visible).

A normal, healthy tree looks like this:

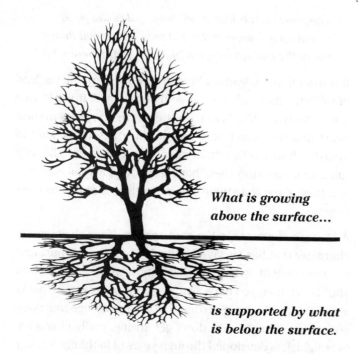

*What is growing
above the surface...*

*is supported by what
is below the surface.*

The size of the part of the tree above ground is directly
proportional to how large the root system is beneath the
ground. You can't have a tiny root system supporting a
great big tree because the thing would simply topple over
the first time any kind of breeze springs up. But enough
for botany lessons!

a) A healthy character

Jesus said:

> *The good man brings good things out of the good stored up in him, and the evil man brings evil things out of the evil stored up in him.* **Matthew 12:35**

It is what is in the leader's heart that will determine the kind of ministry they will have. A godly leader will bring forth a godly ministry. Why? Because they have godliness in their heart and they can't help but produce any other kind of ministry. It would be unnatural for them to do so. The only thing that can stop them having a godly, fruitful ministry is if they allow something evil, something sinful, into their heart.

A leader's character is the root system. If you have godly character that has survived difficulty, temptation, hurt and discouragement, without letting bitterness or cynicism into your heart, then you have a large, strong root system that is able to support a large, strong tree. Just as a huge tree does not grow overnight, you don't get strong, godly character overnight. It is developed through years of faithfully serving God through whatever obstacles the evil one throws in your way, just as James recognized (James 1:2-4).

b) A growing character

If you became a Christian last week, then you probably don't have a large, well-developed root system yet. Don't get depressed about that—no one expects you to have one! But in 10 years time you certainly should have a much larger character base than what you have now.

So a leader who has only been a Christian for a short time will not have a huge, well-developed root system. That's

OK, as long as it is always growing. There is nothing to fear or be embarrassed about if your character is not well developed. The only thing to fear or be alarmed about is when it is not growing. A leader with a small root system will bring forth a small ministry. Like this:

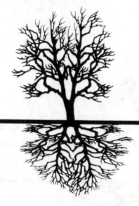

You small but growing ministry...

is supported by your small but growing character.

There is nothing wrong with a small character base as long as it is growing. In fact, there is something wrong with a large, well-developed character that has **stopped** growing! Physically, people stop their main growth after about 20 years, but there is no age or time when your **character** is meant to stop growing! God always wants you to change and become more like him, no matter how long you have been a Christian. You will never completely grow up until you are in heaven. If your character has not become more Christlike in the last year, then something is definitely wrong, regardless of how long you have been a Christian. Of course, the leader who has a growing character will be able to produce a growing ministry!

Therefore the leader who has Christlike character that has survived the test of time has a large root system, and they can support a large ministry or a large area of responsibility within the church. It looks like this:

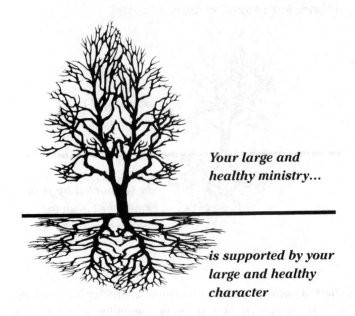

Your large and healthy ministry...

is supported by your large and healthy character

c) An underdeveloped character
The Apostle Paul knew all this, and when he told Timothy who to appoint as leaders, he mentions this warning:

> *He must not be a recent convert, or he may become conceited and fall under the same judgment as the devil.* **1 Timothy 3:6**

What Paul is saying here is to avoid giving great big trees to people with small root systems because he knows that it will result in both the ministry and the leader suffering.

From time to time we can see a large tree put onto someone with a small root system. This could happen when someone is given a large responsibility within the church but they do not have the character to be able to handle it.

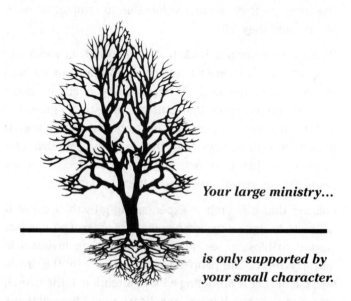

Your large ministry...

is only supported by your small character.

In this situation one of two things will happen. Either the tree will simply topple over and crash to the ground, or else the trunk and branches will shrink back to the size that the roots can support. *(Yeah—this stretches the analogy a bit, but just imagine that trees can do such things!)*

When a tree topples over and collapses, it usually results from a leader doing something that causes their whole ministry to be destroyed—such as committing adultery, or stealing money from the church (or something like that). Probably every one of us has heard of some well-known leader who has been disgraced because they were caught in serious sin. In those cases, people who were very gifted and skilled caused a ministry to grow (that is, the tree was growing to be very large), but their hearts were not growing at the same rate (that is, the roots were being outsized by the tree), so they became vulnerable to temptation, they sinned, and they fell.

When a tree shrinks back to the size that its roots can support, that is where a ministry shrinks and comes back to the size of the leader's heart. There might be some outward circumstance that causes a ministry to grow, but any growth that happens will only remain if the leader is mature enough to have both the skills and the character to do what they have never done before—lead as many people as the growth has caused them to have.

Imagine that a church is experiencing growth because it happens to have a dynamic young preacher who has just started to blossom as he has become more involved in ministry there. The people are encouraged by this fresh, new talent that is attracting a lot of attention. If the overall pastor of the church has a large heart, then they will thank God for this new, young leader and develop him as well as they can. This way the young leader will be even more effective and the church will continue to grow and be blessed by his ministry. Because the pastor's heart is large, the whole ministry will grow.

If, however, the overall pastor feels threatened by this new talent and is upset that it is attracting attention away from their own ministry and preaching, then they will not develop the young leader, they will not give him opportunities to use his gift, and they will not let the church be blessed by his ministry. The young leader will look for, and soon find, opportunities to use his gift elsewhere. He will eventually leave and the church will not grow as it could have if the pastor had a larger and more Christlike heart.

3. Character and skills

All this raises a question: *"Does a leader automatically get a large ministry if they have very Christlike character?"* Well, no! It is God who gives the growth—it is God who produces the fruit in any ministry!

But back to our leader with a Christlike character. Is it enough to simply get your character right, or do you need more?

Think about this: It is not enough to have a great set of tools—you have to know how to use them! If you give some guy walking along the street (let's imagine he is an accountant) a set of top-quality carpentry tools, you can't expect him to automatically produce a masterpiece of woodwork! He might have the tools, but he does not have the skills.

In carpentry, tools are not enough. In ministry, character is not enough. You need skills as well. You must have the character—you will not have fruitful ministry without it—but the skills also need to be present for effective ministry to happen. The good news here is that skills can be learned. Character only comes from a personal relationship with God, but skills can be learned in the same way that you learned to tie your shoelaces, ride a bike or drive a car.

You get character from repentance and faithfulness. You get skills from training and experience.

Note carefully the following formulae:

Character without skills = potential yet to be realised.
The need is for training.

Skills without character = ministry likely to collapse.
The need is for repentance.

Character plus skills = fruitful ministry.
The need is for opportunities to minister.

King David was a man who led God's people with both skills and character for most of his life. 1 Chronicles 18 records a list of nations that David defeated in battle and in return he received lots of money and treasure from them. There is no doubt that when it came to leadership, especially on the field of battle, David had all the skills. The first ten verses of 1 Chronicles 18 describe the kinds of precious metals that were brought to him—gold, silver, bronze, etc.

His tree was growing large because he had great skills in leadership, but all this was happening because God had decided to bless David's ministry. The fact that God was the one who really gave the victory to Israel is a fact acknowledged by both the writer of Chronicles and David himself.

The Lord gave David victory everywhere he went.
1 Chronicles 18:13

David wrote:

If the Lord had not been on our side when men attacked us ... they would have swallowed us alive.
Psalm 124:2-3

It was God who had given David the skills in leadership that he possessed.

However, with all that wealth coming in, it would have been easy for David to decide to spend some of it on the latest mod cons for the royal palace or something like that. Verse 11 tells us what David did decide to do:

> *King David dedicated these articles to the Lord, as he had done with the silver and gold he had taken from all these nations.* **1 Chronicles 18:11**

His character was tested and David passed the test by resisting the temptation to misuse wealth that should have gone to God's temple. After passing the character test, the blessing of God remains on his leadership. Verse 13 tells us that what was happening earlier continues as it repeats the phrase: *"The Lord gave David victory everywhere he went"*. If David had not dedicated the money he had gained from the defeated nations to God, then it is entirely possible that God's blessing might not have remained on his ministry. He might still have been king but he might not have experienced non-stop victory in battle every time he went off to fight.

His tree could have fallen over (God might have raised up a new king to take his place) or else it could have shrunk back down in accordance with the sinfulness of David's heart (Israel could have been defeated and lost much power, wealth, and freedom). If you looked at all this from the outside, if you were there at the time and never had read the biblical account of what was going on, then you would say that Israel was winning battles because David was a very skilful leader, simple as that. But we know from Scripture that David needed both the character and the skills to have the fruitful leadership that he exercised. If he did not have the character, then it would not matter how great his skills were—only God gives lasting fruitfulness, and he does not give it to people who lack character.

4. Invest in your character

Your character is the tool that will make you either a great leader or a lousy leader. You can be a leader who has the character to be able to handle a large, fruitful ministry, or else you can restrict your potential for a lifetime of effective leadership by allowing fear, sin and insecurity to exist in your heart.

Everything that you do for your character will have a positive effect on your usefulness to God in ministry. Every single day that you sit down to spend your regular time with God you are investing in your character and enhancing your potential for leadership. This doesn't mean that we spend time with God for the sole purpose of being able to become a better leader, but one of the undeniable by-products of anything that makes your character more Christlike is that your potential to be used in leadership is raised.

It is always a good decision to invest in your character. If you are tossing up whether or not to go on an expensive conference that will inspire you in your own Christian walk—go! Spend the money! There is nothing more valuable that you can spend your money on! Buy those books, take the time off work to go to that meeting—do it! Any investment in your character is one that will pay good dividends. It is worth the effort to make it happen.

And perhaps even more importantly, make the time to be with God, to pray to him, to read his word, to sing to him, to grow closer to him. It enlarges your heart and sharpens the tool that you will use in leadership. There are few things worse than turning up to ministry after ministry knowing that you are not close to God, that you have sin in your life that needs to be dealt with, that your tool is dull and in need of repair and that your effectiveness in the middle of all this ministry is minimal, despite all the hours you are putting into it.

If a carpenter has been working away for three hours trying to saw a piece of wood with a blunt blade, then you would not call them stupid for taking 15 minutes out to sharpen the blade on the saw before they continue sawing. In fact you would call them stupid for continuing to saw! Sometimes the one thing you need to be more effective in ministry is to get away from all the people you are ministering to, so that you can sharpen your tool for ministry—yourself.

Chapter 9
You are faithful

1. The importance of being faithful

Here is how God has arranged things in leadership: you don't come to Christ one day and then take on leadership of a church of 1000 the next day! You have to mature over time, as we discovered in the last chapter.

Furthermore, as you grow as a Christian, you will begin to get involved in leadership with increasing levels of responsibility. Your very first involvement will probably not be as a senior pastor. It is more likely to be something like helping out with ushering at a church service or helping out with the church youth group or playing a musical instrument—something that does not carry an enormous amount of authority. I believe that God has arranged things this way so that up-and-coming leaders can be tested. God can know what is in your heart, and others will see if you really are faithful. You don't instantly get to great big ministries and huge levels of responsibility without first having to be faithful in serving someone else, and doing tasks that might not seem to be all that significant at the time.

Being faithful is what this chapter is about. The dictionary defines being faithful as being "strict or thorough in the performance of duty" or "true to one's word, promises, etc." **Faithfulness can be defined as simply doing the best you can with what God has given you.** You can't be judged to be faithful if you are not putting a genuine effort into your ministry. The faithful person does their best.

Faithfulness doesn't have anything to do with talent—it is all to do with doing your best and reaching your potential.

If a certain sporting player has much more talent than the people they are playing against, but only puts in a little bit of effort (ie: scores three goals when they could easily have scored six), then they are not faithful. They were not doing their best. If another player in the same game is really quite out of their depth, but tries as hard as they can and doesn't score any goals, then they **are** faithful. They did their best. They scored three fewer goals than the other player, but they were faithful because they did the best that they could with what they had.

Faithfulness, therefore, has nothing to do with what you have, but what you **do** with what you have. Having talent or resources does not make you faithful—it is doing the best that you can regardless of your talent or resources that makes you faithful.

When God looks on a person who does their best when they serve at their ushering post every Sunday morning with enthusiasm and reliability, then he is pleased with the person's faithfulness. When God looks on the ministry of a travelling evangelist who speaks to packed football stadiums every week, doing his best to bring as many people to Christ as possible, he is equally pleased. God desires faithfulness in those who would be in Christian leadership, and he is pleased when he finds it at all levels. He doesn't think that what the usher does is insignificant. He is watching all of his children, and he is looking for faithfulness in everyone, regardless of the size of their task.

Sometimes you are given jobs that don't even get seen by anyone else in the church, so there is little chance that anyone will ever see your ministry—much less thank you for it. At times like that it is so important to remember that God sees your faithfulness. God always notices when people are faithful in ministry. In fact he is looking hard to find people who are faithful.

> *For the eyes of the Lord range throughout the earth to strengthen those whose hearts are fully committed to him.*   ***2 Chronicles 16:9***

God never misses when you are being faithful. He is always watching because he wants to raise up leaders, and he is after those who are faithful in what they have at the moment. The very verse just quoted is given in the context of leadership. The king of Judah, Asa, is being told that his leadership will be cursed with difficulties because he has not been faithful in leading God's way, as he had done in the past.

2. Being faithful in small things

There will be times when you are tempted to think, "Oh well—no one will really notice if I do a lousy job here". This is when you need to remember one important fact: God sees—God **always** sees. He knows who is faithful and who is not, and he knows how faithful you are when no one is looking. God wants you to be faithful right now, when things might be small compared to what you might be doing in the future.

There is an important principle contained in the words of Luke 16:10. This principle says your faithfulness in small things matters. Listen to the words of Jesus:

Whoever can be trusted with very little can also be trusted with much, and whoever is dishonest with very little will also be dishonest with much.

Luke 16:10

The statement is given in the context of teaching about money. If you find that you just can't be generous with your money when you are earning $10 a week, then by the time you are earning $1000 a week you will find it even harder. The person who is generous on a small income will also be generous when they have a large income, and the person who is greedy when they don't have much will still be greedy when they are earning much more. This statement by Jesus strikes right at the heart of the attitude that says, *"I can't give anything right now, but when I am earning more, then I will really be able to contribute."* Jesus knows that that is just not how the human heart works. People who are faithful continue to be faithful as circumstances change, and people who are finding excuses to disobey now will still be finding excuses to disobey long after their original excuse no longer applies.

However, the principle in Luke 16:10 is true in every area of life, and it is certainly true in ministry. If you are not doing your best in your service as an usher, then why would God want to make you the head of the ushering team? If you are not being faithful as a member of the youth leadership team, then you can hardly expect a promotion to the head of that team. That's just not how it works. Everyone knows this.

Imagine that executives at a department store need to promote someone to head of the furniture department. They are hardly likely to look at the various sales staff in that department and say: *"This person here is slack in their work, unmotivated, unreliable and unenthusiastic. It is obvious that they are not cut out for working on the floor. Maybe being department manager is where they would excel. Let's promote them and find out."*

You don't have to be a Christian to have common sense. No one thinks like that! It is most likely that the best person in that department—the most motivated, reliable and enthusiastic—will get the promotion because they have been faithful in the small things. Faithfulness comes before promotion.

What this means is that those who want to be used by God in leadership first have to be faithful in whatever it is that they are doing right now.

If it is being a car-parking attendant in the muddiest corner of the church car park, then you have to be faithful in doing that task. If it is cleaning the toilets after youth group (and that is not a pleasant task!), then make sure that you are giving the youth group the cleanest toilets that you can possibly give them. Let them be bowled over by the sparkle off every single tile! Show them bathrooms so clean that they will not believe that the tiles could be that white. And even if no one at church will see how clean they are (because someone else uses the facility during the week), you work just as hard to make those toilets squeaky clean. Why? Because God sees. Your faithfulness never goes unnoticed by God. He sees you and is proud of you. When you **consistently** have that attitude, God looks forward to giving you more responsibility and moving you on to somewhere where you can be faithful over much.

Notice that the word "consistently" was in the last sentence. It isn't enough to do it once and then think that you have served your time on that particular chore and that you are now a bit above doing things like that. God looks for the attitude that says: *"I am willing to serve. Just let me at it."* That is a whole lot different to the attitude of: *"I'll do it once but don't expect me to keep on doing this"*. Certainly, Jesus didn't think that he was a bit above doing things like dying on a cross. Jesus was faithful even when the task was anything but appealing.

To flat out **refuse** to serve because you think that some task is a bit below you is called "pride". To consistently serve with faithfulness is "humility", and that is the kind of behaviour that God exalts. But to do a task for a little while and then throw it in because you are sick of it is still pride, but now it is wearing a **mask** of humility. God sees straight through the mask immediately. People will also see through the mask, but it will take a little more time for them to see what is really in your heart.

Faithfulness sticks at a task and doesn't give up after it becomes a little bit tiresome. Jesus could have come down off the cross any time he wanted, but his love for you kept him there, and it is that same love that causes leaders to be faithful in serving people even when they find them a bit difficult. Be motivated by Christ's love to be faithful.

If you are working away cleaning the toilets after youth group, or teaching that class of ungrateful children, or whatever it is, think about Jesus. Think about how he was faithful, how he prayed before he was arrested and told

God that he did not really want to go through with what he knew was coming, but still said: *"Yet not my will, but your will be done"*. As you work away at that task that no one sees or no one seems to care about, remind yourself of the faithfulness of Jesus, and determine that you are going to be like him. You are going to have the same determination and commitment that Christ had. You are going to be able to look back and say: *"Just as Jesus was faithful in the task he was given, I have been faithful in the task that I have been given—praise God!"* It is the reminder that Jesus was faithful **then**, and that God sees your faithfulness **now**, that will keep you going.

3. The day of small things

The scene was some 70 years after the destruction of Jerusalem by the Babylonians. The temple—the most important place to all Jews—the place where God himself was present—had been nothing more than ruins for several generations. But at last, God's people had returned from their time in exile. It was time to build a new temple. God wanted the people to do it, and he encouraged them through the prophet Zechariah. Of course, some of the elderly people were just old enough to be able to remember the original temple—the magnificent building that Solomon had inspired the people to construct about 500 years previously. The old temple was IMPRESSIVE with a capital "I". It was something special. The new temple was planned to be a much more ordinary-looking thing. Much smaller, much less imposing. Hardly something to inspire people who had seen the old one in all of its glory.

But that was then and this was now. God was not interested in the past but in getting on with his purposes for this generation. And his will for this generation was that they would build a temple. A small one in comparison, but God has never been too much into comparisons anyway (unlike the elderly people in Zechariah's time!). So God spoke to the people through the prophet Zechariah and asked them:

Who despises the day of small things?
Zechariah 4:10

In the two sentences either side of this quote, God explained that the temple would be finished in this generation and that the people would rejoice because of it. In other words, God's will would be done, and people would be blessed, and that was what really mattered (not comparisons with the past!).

The challenge to the people back then was to not despise the day of small things. You might be someone who has dreams of doing some huge things for God, but right now you are serving away in some ministry, and you wish that someone would hit the fast-forward button so you could get on with some new challenges and opportunities. If that is you, then your challenge is to not despise the day of small things. Don't be upset that you don't have more responsibility than you do right now. Don't get anxious that it might seem that you are being overlooked for chances to do things. Don't despise the day of small things. Instead, focus on being faithful. Faithful in serving the ministries that you are involved in now. Faithful in doing your best to help the people that you have opportunity to help right now. Faithful in teaching the Bible to those you are teaching now. God sees your faithfulness and it is precious to him.

4. God blesses faithfulness

It is important to remember that whatever responsibilities you have now have not fallen upon you by accident. Tasks in ministry come from all sorts of different people and leaders but God is the one who is sovereign over the entire process.

> No one from the east or the west or from the desert can exalt a man. But it is God who judges: He brings one down, he exalts another. **Psalm 75:6-7**

God is the one who will decide whether you will receive the ministry opportunities that you are praying for. Nothing can stop God from raising up someone as a leader, and if you are faithful and obedient to God, then nothing can stand in the way of God blessing your faithfulness.

If you put this fact (that God is the one who raises up people and gives them responsibility) together with what has been mentioned above (how God sees your faithfulness), then you start to see how God works. He blesses faithful people. He promises to. Listen to his very words:

> Those who honour me I will honour. **1 Samuel 2:30**

Simple as that. If you are faithful to God, then he will be faithful to you. He will start to develop the dream he has put in your heart to lead. God blesses faithfulness.

Remember these words:

> We do not want you to become lazy, but to imitate those who through faith and patience inherit what has been promised. **Hebrews 6:12**

Faith and patience are what you need. Don't give up, but have faith and patience.

God will reward your faithfulness. You will never reach a point where the thing you are doing for God is insignificant or where it is too small for him to notice your faithfulness. He always notices, and he always rewards people who are faithful.

Solomon also knew that God can do whatever he wants when it comes to giving people responsibility.

> *The king's heart is in the hand of the Lord; he directs*
> *it like a watercourse wherever he pleases.*
> **Proverbs 21:1**

In this verse God is talking about your leader at church, or about anyone who is in authority over you. Their heart is in the hand of God. God can change their mind on any decision they have made, whenever he wants to. God can cause them to give you all sorts of promotions tomorrow, if he wanted to. So don't hope that all your hard work will be seen by someone important who will be able to mention your name to someone else important and all that—it is God who determines who gets promoted, not you, nor anyone who is leading you, or your church.

This leaves us with some things that need clearing up. You have to let God be God. You can't get upset at God and say to him that he made a bad decision by allowing a particular person to be given a particular job. God can do whatever he wants—he is God and you are not. The issue for you is not *"How on earth did this person come to be put in leadership over me?"* but *"How on earth am I going to respond to this person?"* It is your response that God holds you accountable for.

Your priority is to trust God to bless your faithfulness. He has promised that those who honour him he will honour.

He will promote you in accordance with his will. All you have to do is trust him. God is bigger than any person, any leader, any budget, any decision. If you trust him and are faithful in the small things, then the bigger things will come around in time.

5. Stepping stones

One of the attitudes of a person who doesn't understand faithfulness is that they will only do things as a stepping stone. That is, they will accept doing tasks in ministry for the wrong reasons. The right reason for getting involved in any kind of service within the church is that you love God and you want to help people. But a person who doesn't have faithfulness in their heart will take on a task simply to use it as a "stepping stone" to get to ministry that they **really** want to do. You know if this is the case because when this person is offered a different job, one that they have been wanting to move towards, then they will take the offer up without blinking!

This is tricky ground to negotiate. So let's make a few things clear:

There is nothing wrong with wanting to do something in leadership that you are not doing now. There is nothing wrong with aiming at something different in the future. There is no difficulty with dreaming of a ministry that you might be involved with one day.

Paul told Timothy that to desire to be in church leadership is a good thing (1 Timothy 3:1). If you are currently serving as an assistant youth leader, then there is nothing wrong with hoping that you will one day be **the** youth pastor. What is wrong is when you are not prepared to continue serving as the assistant for as long as God wants you to—when you are more interested in being promoted than you are in loving and serving the people God has put you with now.

A faithful person is much more likely to be sent out to bigger and bolder ministries than someone who is simply using the position as a stepping stone. When an unfaithful person leaves a ministry, the people who have to find a replacement will likely be thinking: *"Well, they have ditched us—hope the next person we get is less selfish than that"*. But when God calls a faithful person to the next thing he wants them to do in ministry, it is more like: *"Wow—I hope so much that God blesses them in the new ministry. They have been such a blessing to us."*

The fundamental difference is that the unfaithful person has their own interests at heart, and this will become obvious to those who need to work with them. However, the faithful person communicates in everything that they do that they have the interests of God's kingdom and God's people at heart.

6. "One-day-when" land

Some leaders live in "one-day-when" land. This is a place where people have all the intentions of being faithful, but for whatever reason they cannot be right now. People who live in "one-day-when" land think things like: *"One day when we have a better pastor, then I'll really serve wholeheartedly at this church"* or: *"One day when I am given more recognition for what I do around here, then I'll really do a top-class job"* or: *"One day when I'm doing something that I'm really gifted at, then I'll try hard"*. These kinds of thoughts are just poorly disguised excuses for not being faithful in the small things. What is more, they are not even good excuses, because the Luke 16:10 principle shows us that the person won't do what they say—if they can't be faithful now, then it is unlikely that they will be faithful under different circumstances.

If you are not doing your best now, serving in the ministry where God has placed, then don't live in "one-day-when" land and make excuses that you are just waiting for something to be different before you start being faithful. Faithfulness starts in the little things, and once it has been established as a part of your character it will most likely stay there, and God will be able to give you more and more ministry responsibility and opportunity.

You don't have to be a brilliant youth leader, but God does call you to be a **faithful** youth leader.

Think through the tasks and ministries that you are responsible for now. How are you going at being faithful?

Chapter 10

You are reliable

One of the key biblical principles of ministry is that we should produce disciples who are able to disciple others, who are able to disciple others, who are able to keep the chain going.

When Jesus came to earth, he didn't try to save as many as he could and then call it a day, taking them all to heaven with him straight away. Sure, Jesus spent time ministering to crowds of people, but it seems that he poured most of his time and energy into making just twelve disciples. He trained these people so that when the Holy Spirit was poured out at Pentecost, they would be able to skillfully lead the rapidly-growing new church.

Jesus' plan was simple: you train those who are gathered around you not only to do their job, but you also empower and equip them to train others, so that they can reproduce themselves in as many people as possible. That way more and more people can be reached for Christ. Because of this strategy of "reproduction", God's saving message has now gone to every country, and every tribe of people. There are disciples being made for Jesus "even to the ends of the earth". All that from Jesus discipling twelve guys for three years!

The idea of reproduction does not just cover the area of discipleship but also the field of leadership. The same method that works so well in making disciples is also

God's method for making leaders. The apostle Paul, who was a great leader, spells this out for us when he gives an instruction to Timothy—one of the leaders whom he had trained and developed himself.

These are Paul's words:

> *And the things you have heard me say in the presence of many witnesses entrust to reliable men who will also be qualified to teach others.*   **2 Timothy 2:2**

You can see in this verse that Paul's concern is that the chain will continue—that the message of his teachings is always being passed on to people, who themselves will pass it on again, and so the chain continues.

1. The condition for reproduction

However, you will notice that Paul puts a **condition** on the kind of people who he wants to be involved in this process. *"Entrust to **reliable** men"* were his words. The condition is that the people will be **reliable**.

The greatest ability in ministry is reliability.

You will learn how true this saying is if you ever have to take responsibility for leading others in a team. If you are the one giving out tasks—and depending on other leaders to pull their weight to help the whole team—then you will know how crucial it is to have **reliable** people on your team (and you'll also know how **frustrating** it is if the people you are depending on are unreliable!). There is nothing worse than having a leader on your team who lets you down and causes the whole ministry to suffer.

The apostle Paul understood how difficult it was to have someone on your team who was not reliable. Certainly we know that Paul had the experience of John Mark deserting the team when Paul and Barnabas had barely started their first missionary journey, something that did not impress Paul at all (Acts 13:13, 15:37-39). People who are not reliable are one of the main sources of frustration for a leader who is depending on others to get things done.

It is something Paul knew, and it is something Solomon knew as well. King Solomon wrote:

> *As vinegar to the teeth and smoke to the eyes, so is a sluggard to those who send him.*   **Proverbs 10:26**

Can you imagine what it is like to have vinegar poured on your teeth? Do you know what it's like to have smoke being blown in your eyes? That's what it's like when people let you down. If someone is a "sluggard" (that is, lazy, half-hearted, and doesn't get their job done), then that is the effect they have on you every time they let you down. Similarly, if you are a member of a ministry team, and you are not being totally reliable, then every time you let your leader down (or let your team down, or let your young people down), it's like pouring vinegar on their teeth, or blowing smoke in their eyes!

Unreliability **always** hurts!

2. The consequences of unreliability

Some people are naturally reliable because that is how they have been brought up. All through school they usually had their homework done, and done by the due date. It might have been a slight rush, but it was done. When they say that they will do something, then you can count on them to do it.

That is what they are like in all areas of life—they are just as reliable in their concert band involvement as in their church involvement as in every thing that they do. They are reliable people, and it is just how they are, and is not necessarily a reflection of their spirituality. When these people's hearts are touched by God and are moved by him to be involved in Christian leadership, then their reliability, which is something they do naturally, is a great blessing to the people that they minister with and minister to.

Other people are not so reliable. They grow up and go through school—sometimes their homework is done and sometimes it isn't, and it all depends on what was on TV last night and how many *Facebook*® friends they were chatting to. They are just not a reliable kind of person. Even so, you can usually get through life without too many problems—unless it's a really severe case of unreliability, where you might lose your job because of chronic absenteeism!

But usually it's not serious things—just an unfortunate well-developed habit of being unreliable, of not finishing the things that you start, of not following through on commitments you make to others, of not being on time, of not being able to be counted on. Of course this kind of person can be a Christian and can love God just as much as anyone else. Sometimes such people are moved by the Holy Spirit to be involved in Christian leadership.

What happens next is that the future of the unreliable leader hits a brick wall when their unreliable nature causes them to be denied the increasing responsibility that they want and that God desires them to have. Up to this point being unreliable has been an annoyance to other people, but it has never had such serious consequences as it does now that the person is involved in Christian leadership.

Solomon was king of Israel for 40 years, so he probably had his fair share of unreliable people working for him. He might have had some of them in mind when he wrote:

> *One who is slack in his work is brother to one who destroys.* **Proverbs 18:9**

They are strong words—words that show the unreliable person what their influence on the world around them is like.

Of course, it depends on what the unreliable person is involved in as to what they actually "destroy". You can look at things like a group assignment at school and think to yourself: *"Who cares if someone's unreliability makes it a bit ordinary?"* But when the person is involved in Christian leadership, then the effectiveness of the ministry and the growth of the kingdom of God are at stake. The difference in importance is huge. What is more, the person probably never really **cared** too much about the results of their group assignments, but because they love God, they really **do** care about effective ministry and the advance of the kingdom of God. But old habits do die hard, and even though they really care, they naturally slip into their unreliable way of life because it is a deeply ingrained way of living—not something that gets changed overnight.

Consider for a moment what you are like when it comes to reliability. When you are assigned something to do, do you carry through with your commitment? Are people surprised when you arrive at something on time? Do you lose important pieces of paper? Are you dependent on others to organise your life and plans? Do you regularly double-book yourself? Do you finish the projects that you start? The answers to questions like these will tell you if you are a reliable person or not.

Of course, in reality, there are not just reliable people and unreliable people—there is a spectrum with people spread from one extreme to another with every possible shade of grey in between. Probably all of us could be more reliable than we are now, but some of us obviously need to take action more immediately than others. Those are the people who are "destroying" the ministry they are involved in with their slackness.

3. Taking action

a) Realise how serious this is

If you are a person who is consistently unreliable, then the first thing that you need to do is **realise the seriousness of your position**. Your whole potential as a leader of God's people is under threat from your unreliability. Paul told Timothy **only** to train reliable people for ministry. If Timothy was in your church, and was looking around for reliable people so he could train them for future ministry and leadership—would he pick you?

Every leader who has ever led a team ministry knows how bad it is to be let down by unreliable people! So they are drawn to reliable people, sometimes consciously and sometimes unconsciously. The greatest ability in ministry is reliability, and until you have that ability it doesn't matter how many other abilities you have.

Being reliable really matters!

b) Start the process of change

The next step is to **begin the often long process of changing the way that you behave**. This might be the first time in decades that this particular well-entrenched way of living has been challenged. It may not go without a fight.

Here's what happened to John Warren, a guy who used to work with me in my youth-ministry team:

One of the habits that I had to confront and deal with was procrastination in study. For the last five years of my six years at high school I had grown gradually slacker and slacker in my attitude to my studies. In my final year you could find me working away in the library at 2:45pm if the assignment was due at 3:00pm. I took the term "last minute" to new dimensions. This did not particularly worry me because I was much more interested in other things going on in my life. It should have worried me, because I knew full well that Colossians 3:23 says to work at everything with all your heart, as if working for the Lord. I chose to disobey and become slack. I was a classic example of an unmotivated student.

Not long after leaving high school a dream came true and I started studying at Bible college. I was now the most motivated student in the world—it was just too good to be true that I was able to prepare for ministry in this exciting and challenging way. I was supremely confident that because my motivation had changed, I would find it easy to get those assignments done in plenty of time.

One month later my confidence lay shattered as I slaved over the computer at 2 am the night before *an assignment was due. I could not believe that even though I now really **did** care about what I was doing, I couldn't shake the old habits of slackness that had formed during my unmotivated time of study. But I had been taught about being reliable and disciplined so I knew it was time to change. This is how I progressed over two years of studying:*

First semester—most assignments finished at 1am the night before they were due.

Second semester—most assignments finished at 9pm the night before they were due.

Third semester—most assignments handed in one day before they were due.

Fourth semester—most assignments handed in one week before they were due.

It was a process, but I made it. I was changed, and the change had to happen for me to keep moving forward as the leader God wanted me to be.

For you it might be a shorter process or it might be a longer one, or it might be something that you don't really need to go through because you have always been pretty reliable. For those of you who realise that you are unreliable and you do need to change, then you are standing at the start of an exciting process—a process where God will change you so that you can realise the plan that he has for your life. It is an exhilarating thing to get on top of something that you thought would be very difficult to conquer!

4. A commitment made

Being reliable is all about the **little things**; like phoning ahead to say that you can't make the meeting because of a family commitment, and phoning as soon as you are informed about the meeting, not 10 minutes before it starts.

One other aspect of reliability is **keeping your word**. King David makes this clear in Psalm 15. This is a psalm where David asks a question about which people are fit to be with God. The entire psalm answers that question by giving a list of the qualities that characterise the righteous person. They include things like *"speak the truth from your heart"*, and other qualities such as generosity. In verse four David describes the righteous person as being someone *"who keeps his oath even when it hurts"*. That has real implications for people who want to be reliable.

In your week-in, week-out involvement in ministry, you make many commitments to people that you don't think too carefully about before you make them. You say things such as: *"I'll pray for you"*, *"I'll give you a call"*, *"I'll be there at 7:30"*. When you say those things, you are making a promise to someone—you are promising them that you will pray, or that you will make that call, or that you will take whatever action that you have committed yourself to.

Never take such promises lightly. The psalmist describes the holy person as someone who keeps their oath **even when it hurts**. If you have said that you will be there at 7:30, then don't let anything stop you from fulfilling that commitment. People expect you to keep your word, and you will erode their trust in you if you do not keep your promises. Of course, if something unexpected does come up, then you must phone and let people know what the problem is!

If you break small promises such as these, then do not think nothing of it. People can rationalise that kind of disobedience by saying: *"That's just the way I am"* or: *"It doesn't really matter"*. It does matter, and if it is the way that you are, it is because that is who you have chosen to become. You now need to change your decision and become someone different, someone who keeps their oath, even when it hurts. If you make any commitment to someone, then you have to do everything within your power to ensure that you keep your word to that person.

There will most likely be times when you have said something that you should not have—you have promised someone that you will do a particular task, when you really should have let someone else do it. You then realise that there are only 24 hours in the day, and you can't get everything done!

When you find that you have trapped yourself by making a commitment that you simply can't keep, then you have two options open to you.

The first one, and the best one, is to simply work as hard as you can and maybe miss a little sleep or relaxation, in order to meet the various commitments you have made with your words. Then you can sit down and resolve never to make such hasty and poorly-thought-through decisions again!

The second option is to simply go to someone as soon as you have worked it out and say: *"I said I would do this but I simply cannot. Sorry. Please forgive me."* Either way, you need to make sure that you do not make the same mistake again, and that you think carefully before you take a commitment on. Once you have promised with your mouth to do something, then people's trust in you will be eroded if you don't do it.

To be a candidate for leadership you have to be a reliable person. Habits of slackness that might have existed in your life up to this point must be removed if you are to reach the potential that you have as a leader within the kingdom of God.

The greatest ability is reliability. When others describe you, would they naturally use the word "reliable" to show what you're like? If God were looking for **reliable** people to train for further ministry and leadership, would he pick you?

Chapter 11

You are a follower

1. Why authority exists

Imagine for a moment what human civilisation would be like if there were no governments, rulers, kings, councils, or authorities of any kind. No police, no courts, no justice, no prisons, or any kind of law enforcement. Imagine that no parents had any control over their children. The kids simply did whatever they wanted to. Imagine there were no rules or discipline in any schools, and students could do anything they felt like. Imagine bosses had no power to control their workers, who could do anything while they were on the job. Imagine that people simply did whatever they wanted to, and that no human authority could bring anyone to account for anything that they had done.

Sound like a recipe for chaos? If there were no authorities, then our entire planet would disintegrate into anarchy, and nothing worthwhile would get done!

That is definitely not the will of God for our race, so God has taken steps to make sure that this kind of chaos does not happen. What God has decided to do is to place human authorities over people, so that leaders (ie: those in authority) can create and maintain order and peace. God has put all kinds of different authorities in different parts of society—he has put authorities (ie: leaders) over nations, over families, over churches, over schools, over cities and all sorts of other parts of society.

Paul tells us this in Romans 13:

> *Everyone must submit himself to the governing*
> *authorities, for there is no authority except that which*
> *God has established. The authorities that exist have*
> *been established by God.*   **Romans 13:1**

This verse clearly tells us that there is no government leader, and there is no church leader, who has come to power except for the will of God. Every authority has been placed there by God—and the start of the verse says that we are to submit to those authorities.

God is the supreme authority. God can place people in authority because he is the ultimate authority himself. Why? Because everyone, including leaders, will one day stand before God to give an account to him of what they have done with their life, and God will judge them. God is the greatest authority, and he has delegated his authority to various people on earth—politicians, leaders, parents, pastors, etc.

At the moment you have a number of authorities over you. You are a citizen of your country, so you are under the authority of your respective government. If your government says that you are only allowed to drive at a particular speed on the roads, then you submit to that rule and keep to the speed limit. If you live at home, you are under the authority of your parents, so if they say, *"Clean up the house"*, then you should do it, regardless of whether you want to or not, because you are under their authority. If you are a part of a local church, then you are under the authority of the pastor and the leaders of that church, so when they say that the church is heading in this particular direction, you submit and support them. You don't do this because you necessarily think it is a great decision (you may or may not), but you submit because you are a person under spiritual authority.

Christians affirm and agree with the truth that God is the supreme authority because we know that God is perfect and that he will judge people with complete justice. We do not fear that God will make mistakes when he uses his authority—we know that God is perfectly loving and does not make mistakes. That is easy to handle. But people being given authority? People are sinful—all of them. People make mistakes. People are capable of being extremely cruel to others. If you give authority to people, then they are sure to abuse that authority and millions may suffer as a result.

Anyone who knows the first thing about world history knows that it is true that people abuse authority. We can understand that God would want us to submit to good leaders who generally do what is right, but what about people like Hitler? Surely God can't expect us to submit to people like him!

Paul continues in Romans 13:

> *Consequently he who rebels against the authority is*
> *rebelling against what God has instituted, and those*
> *who do so will bring judgement on themselves.*
> **Romans 13:2**

There is no room for exception here (Scripture does allow us one exception, but we will come to that later on). What is more, Paul wrote those words when the government of the day cruelly persecuted Christians. It is not as though Paul never knew what a bad human authority looked like!

2. Who is accountable to whom?

Of course, God cares deeply when people abuse the authority that he has given them, and he is upset when innocent people suffer because of the sinfulness of someone in authority. God does not sit idly by, taking no notice of such things. All people who hold any kind of authority— and that includes you if you hold any kind of leadership position in your church—will answer to God for how they have used their authority. Hitler himself will stand before God to be judged on how he used his authority (and you may suspect that he will be judged harshly). If you have a leader at church, or anywhere in your life, who is **not** doing a good job, then that person will answer to God for what they are doing.

Of course the problem that you face right now is knowing how to respond to a leader who is **not** doing the job that you think God wants them to be doing. It is well and good to know that one day they will have to give an account to God, but you have to deal with a situation right now, when the Day of Judgment might not be coming next week!

What you need to know is that you are accountable to God for how you respond to all the authorities over you, be they good or bad. You can respond with obedience or with rebellion, and God holds you accountable for the response you choose, regardless of whether your leader is Mother Teresa or Adolf Hitler himself. The leader is accountable for how they use the authority that God has given them, and the follower is accountable for how they respond to the leader, regardless of how good or bad the leader is. If you have a bad leader, and you respond with rebellion, then you have sinned and God holds you accountable for that.

We saw earlier in the chapter on faithfulness that God sees the hearts of people and he chooses who to promote and who not to promote (Psalm 75:6-7). What this means is that we leave the promoting to God—that is his job. Our job is to submit to whichever leader God places over us. If you choose to leave the promoting to God, then it means that you would never take part in a rebellion against a leader. You are commanded to submit—always.

To rebel against a leader would be to take on the role of God; for he is the one who removes leaders. If I were living under the rule of someone like Hitler, then I might pray for their downfall or their repentance, but I would not lift a finger to hurt the man. God can remove him any time he wants to. He does not need me to play God and do it for him.

So, to summarise:

The leader: accountable for how they use their authority.

The follower: accountable for how they respond.

The leader: is to use their authority to do good.

The follower: is to submit regardless of the quality of leadership.

3. What David did

All of this theory makes more sense when you put skin and bone on it and see it working in practice. One of the most wonderful examples of submission in the Bible is that of David when he was under the rule of the evil king, Saul. David was the most loyal and submissive of subjects, but despite all this, King Saul was jealous of what David did on the battlefield. This jealousy expressed itself in the most sinister of ways. Saul, in a fit of rage, tried to kill David by pinning him to the wall with his spear. David had no choice but to flee for his life. Saul would not rest with David out of his house—the chase was on. Saul took an army of 3000 men and began to hunt David down, bent on killing him.

One day, David was hiding in a cave with some of his followers, and Saul with his army was just outside the cave, but he did not know that David was inside. Things then got really interesting when Saul decided to duck inside the cave to go to the bathroom. David's followers could not believe their good luck—the evil king had unknowingly wandered into their hideout on his own. All of them urged David to take a knife and creep up and kill Saul; they even said that God had brought Saul there for that very reason.

David was faced with a choice, to kill Saul or not—the very person who had tried on many occasions to kill him.

> *David crept up unnoticed and cut off a corner of*
> *Saul's robe.*   ***1 Samuel 24:4***

That's all. Just took a bit of his robe. He didn't lay a finger on the man, because he knew that God wanted him to submit to the leaders over him, even the evil ones, even the ones who might try to kill him. To those who were urging him to kill Saul, David turned and said:

> *The LORD forbid that I should do such a thing to my*
> *master, the Lord's anointed, or lift my hand against*
> *him; for he is the anointed of the LORD.*
> ***1 Samuel 24:6***

You will notice that David's reason for not attacking Saul had nothing to do with how well or unwell Saul was doing as king. David had chosen to submit because he knew it was right, not because he thought Saul was doing a great job as king.

When Saul had left the cave, still completely oblivious to what had happened, David came out and shouted to get the attention of Saul and his men. He held up the piece of robe and told Saul how he could have killed him, but chose not to because Saul was God's anointed leader.

David said to Saul:

> *May the LORD judge between you and me. And may the LORD avenge the wrongs you have done to me, but my hand will not touch you. As the old saying goes, "From evildoers come evil deeds," so my hand will not touch you.*   **1 Samuel 24:12-13**

David knew that removing leaders was God's job and that God didn't need help from him, so he refused to oppose Saul even though it was obvious that David would have been a better king than Saul. The response of Saul to having his life spared by the man he was trying to kill was to simply be ashamed of what he was doing, and to go home, leaving David in peace.

Unfortunately it was only temporary, and Saul's foolishness returned to him. A short time later he was hunting David once more. Just two chapters later in 1 Samuel 26 a similar incident happened all over again. This time David and one of his followers sneaked into Saul's poorly-guarded camp and took the spear and water jug that were lying near Saul's head as he slept. David's follower, Abishai, urged him to put the spear straight through Saul's heart.

David responded:

> *Don't destroy him! Who can lay a hand on the Lord's anointed and be guiltless?*   **1 Samuel 26:9**

Once again David let Saul live. Not because he deserved to live but because it was right to let him live.

David submitted to someone who was obviously evil and out of control. Now you probably have not had someone like that in authority over you! But we all have had imperfect people who make mistakes in authority over us. Often it is easy to submit when we agree with the decision that has been made, but what is really in our hearts comes out when a decision is made that we do not agree with. Will you do something your pastor asks, even if you don't want to, even if you think it is a stupid idea, even if you would do it differently yourself? David would, because he was submissive. Whether or not you will follow in David's footsteps will be seen when you are asked to do something you don't want to do.

You cannot have David's attitude if you join with others in criticising and bad-mouthing leaders (even leaders who are doing an obviously bad job). The submissive person would not do that. Submission works everywhere, not just at church. So not only do I not gossip about or slander church leaders, but I also choose not to deride and abuse political leaders. In many Western nations "politician bashing" is practically a national sport; but it has rebellion, not submission, at its heart. It follows that if we don't submit to our political leaders, we will have difficulty in submitting to our church leaders. Rebellion starts with words and then becomes actions. I want to be submissive in both what I say and what I do.

4. What Jesus did

David's submission to Saul is a wonderful example to us, but the ultimate picture the Bible gives us of submission is that of the Son to the Father.

Jesus told his disciples for many years that he was going to face his death in Jerusalem at the hands of his enemies. He knew that the cross was in store for him. Crucifixions were very common at that time in history, so all throughout his childhood Jesus would have seen various criminals hanging on crosses. It would have been a regular reminder to him (at least during the three years of his ministry, if not his entire life) of what he would face one day.

Jesus did not want to be crucified. He knew that the pain would be simply incredible—for him it was a moment-by-moment decision to stay up there and endure the pain, because with one command an army of angels could have rescued him. But he stayed there and chose not to make that command.

Jesus also knew that God the Father wanted him to be crucified. There was no doubt about that—he had known it for years. So for Jesus everything came to a head one evening just a few hours before his death. He knew that Judas, his betrayer, could arrive at any minute, bringing the party that would arrest him. The trial and the execution would follow swiftly. He had but a few moments to talk to his Father and seek strength to endure what was coming.

Jesus and his disciples were in a garden together, and he told them:

> *My soul is overwhelmed with sorrow to the point of death.* **Matthew 26:38**

What an amazingly difficult time that must have been! To talk about being overwhelmed even to the point of death is strong language. It was not just the pain and suffering of the crucifixion itself that Christ had to contend with (as if that were not enough)! He also had to deal with the role of being the sin-bearer of the whole world; being the one on whom the judgment of God was falling, even though he was not guilty himself; being the one who had always enjoyed the most perfect and intimate relationship with God, which was about to be smashed. Jesus stood before the enormity of that task and said that he was overwhelmed, to the point of death. He did not want to do it.

So he left the disciples, and prayed on his own. He fell onto the ground, face down, and said:

> *My Father, if it is possible, may this cup be taken from me. Yet not as I will, but as you will.* **Matthew 26:39**

Such a simple prayer—acknowledging that he did not want to do this—but he was choosing to be submissive. He would submit his will to that of the Father, even though it would cost him his life. That is the most wonderful example of submission that mankind will ever know. Where would you and I be if the Son had not chosen to submit to the will of the Father? Yet because he did, there is now hope for every single person on this planet, to be forgiven and have eternal life.

The essence of submission is choosing the will of the person in authority rather than your own. When you are involved in leadership in the local church, there will always be times when your leader will ask you to do something in a way that you would rather not do. Even if you think that your leader and you are the two most like-minded people in the world, with the passing of time there will eventually come an area where you disagree, and you will have to choose to submit or to resist. The examples of David and Jesus show us what to do.

5. When there is disagreement

Being submissive does not mean that you never let your leader know that you have a different opinion. To explain how you should go about approaching your leader when there is a disagreement, let's use an imaginary example.

Imagine you are the assistant youth pastor at your church. You are directly under the authority of the main youth pastor for everything that you do in your ministry. Together you run a successful Friday-night youth group as you seek to minister the gospel to the young people in the area. Imagine that one day the youth pastor comes to you and says that while it has been good having Friday-night youth groups, he feels that we would be better served and would see more fruit if we moved our programme to a Saturday evening. The move is on! Friday night to Saturday night!

Your reaction is one of horror! As you think about the issues, you are convinced that this will be a **terrible** move for your youth ministry. You are certain that fewer young people will come, that fewer leaders will be available, that there will be less fruit, there will be a loss of momentum, and that the entire group could even grind to a halt!

You spend time in prayer on the issue. The more that you pray and think about it, the more you become convinced that your youth pastor is on the verge of making an awful decision—one that will seriously retard the spread of the gospel among the youth in your area. The youth pastor is convinced that the reverse will happen and that the ministry will flourish. But you are certain that he is wrong. You are both strongly persuaded that your own point of view is correct.

A few things should be pointed out about this situation. Firstly, the problem is not with anyone's motives. No one here is slack in their desire to serve God. No one has a bad attitude. Both of the parties involved have the spread of the gospel at heart and are united in their desire to make disciples of young people. There is no disagreement about the desired outcome of the ministry—the disagreement is about the best way to **reach** that outcome.

Secondly, this is not the kind of situation where you can open your Bible and find out what to do. If there was an obedience or an attitude problem, then you could check what the Bible said, but that is not the case. You could read your Bible non-stop for ten years and you would still not be one inch closer to solving the problem. All your Bible will tell you to do is to love God and make disciples. It will not tell you if you should make disciples with a Friday-night programme or a Saturday-night programme!

This is not the kind of situation that you can just sweep under the carpet. It is an important decision and if you are right, then for the sake of the gospel, you must persuade the youth pastor to change his mind. In short, you two have to talk about it—and that is always the first step you should take when you disagree with your leader.

Step 1: Appeal

In our imaginary scenario, the first step you should take is to go to your youth pastor and say that you have prayed about the matter and you really believe that for all these reasons, we should stay on a Friday night. You would probably try as hard as you could to persuade him to change his mind. If you really do have the right point of view on the matter, then it is important that you do everything you can to help the youth pastor see your side of the disagreement. We would talk over the various factors involved in making the decision. The youth pastor might allow you a lot of time to express yourself, or he might not be very interested at all.

It is important to realise that if you are being submissive, then you cannot briefly appeal to your leader, and then go and complain to someone else about what a lousy leader you have! The correct first step is to appeal, but to also keep a positive attitude towards your leader. You might acknowledge to other people that you are working through the possibility of moving the program to a Saturday night, but you cannot speak badly of your leader. This is a difficult, "greyish" kind of area, (knowing what to say and what not to say to others about what is happening) so here is a good general rule: **Do not say anything about your leader behind their back that you would not be comfortable in saying right to their face**. It is difficult to go wrong if you keep to that rule, and are determined to honour the person that God has placed in authority over you.

As well as appealing directly to your leader, you should pray that they would change their mind.

> *The king's heart is in the hand of the Lord; he directs*
> *it like a watercourse wherever he pleases.*
>
> *Proverbs 21:1*

God can change the mind of any leader on any matter, regardless of whether they have held that opinion for the last 50 years or 5 minutes. What is more, God honours submissive people, so if you do have the right opinion on a certain issue, and you are going about it in the right way, then pray with confidence that God will change the mind of the person in authority.

So, in our example, you go to your youth pastor and explain your case. He listens patiently, thanks you for your input, and then, to your disappointment, he says that he is sure that God will bless a Saturday-night programme, so the change is still on.

What do you do next?

Step 2: Submit anyway OR leave
The time for appealing has come and gone. The youth pastor's mind has not been changed. If his decision is a bad one, then he will account to God for it. You have done everything that you can do to warn him of the dangers. Any week now, your Friday programme will cease, and the Saturday one will start. If you are to be a submissive follower, then you have two choices.

The first is simply to **submit anyway**. If you choose this option, then you decide that you will do everything that you can to make the Saturday-night programme as successful and fruitful as possible. You will acknowledge to yourself that this is probably not the way that you would do it if you were the youth pastor, but God has placed you here to serve your youth pastor's vision, so you will do so with all of your energy.

It is not good enough to simply go along to a Saturday-night programme but not give it your best. If you were to be there with a frown on your face, dragging your feet and crying, *"I told you so!"* at the first sign of any difficulties, then you are not being submissive.

That is like the rebellious child who refused to be seated when her teacher asked her to. After a long and heated conflict, the child had to sit down but said as she was doing it: *"I'll sit down, but I am standing up on the inside!"*

Submission is when you say to an authority (as Christ did): *"Yet not as I will, but as you will"*. When Jesus went to the cross, he was not *"standing up on the inside"*—he was completely submissive to the will of his Father. The first of your two options is to bite the bullet and do everything that you can possibly do to make Saturday night a roaring success. Any halfhearted attempt is not submission at all. It is *"standing up on the inside"*.

Here is your second option—**you leave**. You go to your youth pastor and explain that you cannot support a Saturday-night youth programme (for the reasons already explained), so you are withdrawing from your position of leadership. You don't leave with bitterness or with slanderous words on your tongue. You simply leave wishing your youth pastor all the best in the new programme. You pray for him, you pray that God will bless the new venture, and you are delighted if it does bear fruit. But because of your feelings on the whole issue, you choose to withdraw yourself from being under your youth pastor's spiritual authority.

You definitely do not go and start up an independent youth group on a Friday night! That is outright rebellion. It is standing up on both the inside and the outside! And of course, you steadfastly refuse to badmouth or denigrate the character of your youth pastor!

If you are currently facing a situation where you feel you are up to step two, then please try again to take option one. Submission really only begins when we choose to do something that we don't want to do. Submission is Christlike. When we choose to submit in a situation, then a little bit more of the character of Christ is developed in us.

God sometimes uses conflict situations to move people onto the next thing that he has for them. Sometimes it is the right decision to leave a church, or leave a particular ministry after a disagreement has arisen. But if at all possible, try to submit! It is **always** the preferred option. If we always parted company with everyone we had a disagreement with, then we would not get far in life, and the Christian church would not do much effective ministry!

Sometimes disagreements arise because of opinions on ministry matters (like the example we have been considering), and sometimes disagreements arise because of personality differences. Two people find that they don't work well together—they have a personality clash. Either one or both parties feels that the partnership in ministry cannot continue. So much of ministry is learning how to work with people. If you are caught in a disagreement, try and take option one and submit anyway, but especially so if you are caught in a disagreement that is personality based. There will always be people who have personalities that sometimes clash with yours. We have to learn how to work with those people. The advance of the gospel is at stake here—we cannot afford to let our own tastes and preferences get in the way of what God wants us to do. If your disagreement is personality based, then take option one, not option two.

Paul's words are appropriate in this context:

> *Submit to one another out of reverence for Christ.*
> **Ephesians 5:21**

6. The exception

There is one exception—one instance where it is right for us to deliberately disobey an authority. This is shown to us in the Acts of the Apostles when Peter and John are preaching away and causing quite a stir all around the city. They are told by the authorities to stop preaching about Jesus, because of the trouble that it is causing for the rulers who were threatened by the explosion of Christianity that had just started. Peter and John have a choice to either obey this earthly authority or to obey the command of Jesus to spread the word of his death and rising. They could not obey both, because the two commands were in direct contradiction. So they say to the rulers who want them to stop preaching:

> *Judge for yourselves whether it is right in God's sight*
> *to obey you rather than God. For we cannot help*
> *speaking about what we have seen and heard.*
> **Acts 4:19-20**

They disobeyed an earthly authority because they were told not to do something that the Bible says they **must** do. That is the exception. You can and should disobey an authority when you are told to disobey a command of Scripture. This is the case because God is the supreme authority; he is over every earthly authority. So Peter and John kept on preaching, and Christians today continue to defy earthly authority when it goes against the clear command of God in the Bible. While we must be prepared to do such things, they should not be done with a reckless attitude that seeks opportunities to rebel. They should be done with a simple commitment to obeying Jesus.

7. Make your leader's job a joy

When the Bible teaches us about authority, it does not just give us wisdom for what we should do when there is a disagreement. Fortunately it also tells about the attitude that we should have all the time, both when relationships are harmonious and when they are not. The clearest example of this is a short command that the writer to the Hebrews gives us. He says:

> *Obey your leaders and submit to their authority. They watch over you as men who must give an account. Obey them so that their work will be a joy, not a burden, for that would be of no advantage to you.*
>
> **Hebrews 13:17**

That verse does not tell us much that we have not already looked at in this chapter, but look at that phrase, *"a joy, not a burden"*. Think for a moment of your leader, the one person at your church who is the most directly responsible for either your ministry or your own spiritual growth. Consider that person, put yourself in their shoes, and think about you from their point of view. As they consider you, do you think that you are a joy or a burden to them? The submissive person is not simply agreeable but they are a joy to their leader. When their leader considers them, the first thought that crosses their mind is a positive one!

If Jesus has called you to be a **leader,** you must first realise that he has also called you to be a **follower**. Not just a follower of Jesus, but a follower of those in rightful authority over you. He calls upon you to show Christlike and joyful **submission** to those placed in authority over you.

So think about how you treat the various "authorities" in your life—the government, your bosses, your teachers, your parents (if you live at home with them), your sports coach, your youth pastor, your senior pastor—all of them! Think about the attitude you have towards them, **especially when you disagree with them**!

Does "joyful submission" describe your attitude? Do you do everything you can to make their work a joy, not a burden?

How would you feel if YOUR attitude to those in authority was duplicated by your young people in the way they respond to you?

1. The problem of "leadership qualities"

What would you say are the qualities of a good leader? If you had to list the attributes of someone who led well, what would you write down? When you think about a picture of someone with strong leadership, what comes to your mind?

This could be a national leader, or a sporting captain, or a leader of industry, or a school captain, in fact any sort of leader. What sort of qualities does a successful leader need to possess?

Here are some of the popular answers that people give me to this question:

Strong personality... visionary... methodical... knows their purpose... sticks to their guns... brings change... able to encourage loyal followers... achieves their objectives... good public speaker... able to influence others' thinking... takes decisive action... takes responsibility... delegates well... has a chain of command... rewards their followers... admired by many... inspires the multitudes... deals with those who oppose them... makes everyone think "we want this"... inspires pride... achieves success... ensures commitment... follows through... removes obstacles to the plan... develops a team... and so the list goes on!

A pretty impressive bunch of qualities! I think that **I** would be impressed with anyone who displayed that catalogue of outstanding talents! But if lists like the one above were the **only** judge of how good a leader is, I want to suggest we are missing something crucial!

Let me explain what I mean. How would Adolf Hitler stack up as a leader against the above list?

Come on—look again at the list. How does Adolf Hitler stack up as a leader? You can put a big "tick" next to nearly every quality! He had a strong personality... he had a vision... he was methodical... he knew his purpose... he stuck to his guns... he brought change... he encouraged loyal followers... and so the list goes on. On every examination you would have to say that Hitler **excelled** at nearly every quality of being a leader! If you go by the above list, you would have to conclude that Hitler was one of the **greatest leaders** of the twentieth century!

But there might be something within you that is saying: "No—this can't be right! Surely Hitler was a **bad** leader! Look at all the evil he caused! Look at all the people he killed! Look at all the turmoil in the world that he caused! What do you mean, Hitler was a **good** leader?"

That all depends on what you think makes someone a good leader. The list above only talks about **skills** and **abilities**. That's what we usually think of when we think about leadership qualities. On the "skills and abilities test", Hitler was a superb leader.

But as you have probably discovered from the preceding chapters, leadership is not just about **skills**—it's also about **character**. If we put Hitler through the "character test", he fails miserably. He was decidedly evil. We would have been better off if he had never existed. He brought unspeakable evil into our world.

If you are a Christian youth leader, then you will want to match up to what **God** thinks is a great leader. We started the chapter by thinking about the qualities that would make someone a good leader. If we now look at the New Testament, what leadership qualities does the **Bible** give for those who would lead in Christ's name?

2. Biblical leadership qualities

There are four places in the New Testament where the qualities of a biblical leader are listed. You will see a summary of these lists in Appendix 1 on page 295 . They make for very interesting reading. **They are a very different list from what we started with at the outset of this chapter!**

Here are the four lists. Why don't you take a moment to look through them by yourself? They are addressed to four different groups of people, called "overseers", "deacons", "the Lord's servant" and "elders". But don't let the titles worry you—all four of these categories are people who are **leaders** in God's church.

Close this book right now. Don't read ahead. *(It's okay—I'll still be here when you come back!)* Look up these passages by yourself, and see what you notice:

- *1 Timothy 3:1-7*

- *1 Timothy 3:8-13*

- *2 Timothy 2:22-26*

- *Titus 1:5-9*

Okay, what did you notice?

I'll tell you what I noticed! There are many, many personal **character** qualities identified, but only **one skill** mentioned. To put that another way—my English translation of these four passages uses 321 words to describe the personal character qualities, and only 84 words to describe the skills. I don't think that God is trying to give us a maths lesson here, but 80% of what God wants to say to leaders concerns their character, and 20% concerns their skill of teaching the Bible well.

It's interesting how these lists are interpreted by others. I know of one Bible college which says: *"There's only one skill mentioned in the biblical lists—to teach the Bible well—so that's what we'll devote most of our attention to"*. That Bible college produces good Bible teachers who are often sadly lacking in the development of their Christian character!

I know of another Bible college which looks at exactly the same biblical lists, and concludes: *"Most of God's emphasis is on developing character—so that's what we'll devote most of our attention to"*. That Bible college produces students of exceptional Christlike character, whose ability to teach the Bible well is often sadly lacking!

Lets have a look at what God's standard is for leadership—so that you might check out how you are going by this biblical standard.

3. The one skill you must have!

There are probably many skills that a youth leader should have. You need to be able to organise. You need to be able to listen. You need to know how to comfort those in distress. You need to plan and run a youth ministry budget. You need to know how to delegate and organise your volunteers. You need to be a reasonable public speaker. It helps if you can play the guitar (or at least own a van!).

But the Bible only mentions **one skill** for those who would be leaders in God's church. Just one skill. One ability. One "thing" that you have to be able to get right. All the other skills mentioned above (plus a whole stack more that we haven't got room to list here!) are all useful. They are all helpful. There are all sorts of courses that you can go on to help develop these skills to make you more effective.

But in among all these helpful skills, there is one skill that stands out as being **absolutely essential**. One ability that every Christian leader needs to have to one degree or another. One task that is highlighted in almost every list in the Bible that is essential for every leader.

Just one. Here it is:

You need to be able to teach the Bible well.

Able to teach…   *1 Timothy 3:2, 2 Timothy 2:24*

> *Those who oppose him he must gently instruct, in the*
> *hope that God will grant them repentance leading*
> *them to a knowledge of the truth.*   ***2 Timothy 2:25***

> *He must hold firmly to the trustworthy message as it*
> *has been taught, so that he can encourage others by*
> *sound doctrine and refute those who oppose it.*
>   ***Titus 1:9***

> *Until I come, devote yourself to the public reading of*
> *Scripture, to preaching and to teaching.*
>   ***1 Timothy 4:13***

A Christian leader is not essentially someone who runs activities for an organisation. In youth ministry, we are not primarily called to run child-minding or a welfare agency. We might do **lots** of these things as secondary activities, but as leaders we are mainly called on by God to teach his word faithfully.

This takes us to the very heart of what Christian ministry is. We are to be used by God in any way he sees fit, so that other people might be changed and impacted by his word—so that they will become the people that he has designed them to be.

How will people be changed and impacted by God's word? It's very simple, really. **We** teach them! We might teach God's word to audiences of thousands; we might lead a small Bible-study group; we might teach people in a one-to-one situation, either in a pastoral relationship or with individual discipling. But if there's one thing we need to make sure that we get right, then it is to teach God's word—boldly, gently, and faithfully.

Some people are "natural teachers"—others are a little more hesitant in this area. But with our differing personalities, and different spiritual gifts, and various natural inclinations and divergent styles, every Christian leader is called on to play his or her part in ensuring that God's word is taught faithfully to the incoming generation. That is the essence of youth ministry. What a privilege!

Do you need to be reminded of the absolute importance of teaching God's word? Then turn back to Chapter 5—"Task 2: Feed your sheep".

Do you want to learn some "how-to's" in the area of Bible teaching? Then check out the information in Chapter 14.

But whatever you do, work at it! Become a skilled workman when it comes to teaching God's word. It will be a huge benefit to you—and a huge benefit to the young people you lead.

> *Do your best to present yourself to God as one*
> *approved, a workman who does not need to be*
> *ashamed and who correctly handles the word of truth.*
> ***2 Timothy 2:15***

4. The one quality you must have

The Bible gives us many personal qualities so you can check up on how you are going in the leadership stakes. (More about them in the next chapter!) But there is one quality which is at the head of the list, because it overrides and controls all the other personal characteristics.

Check it out:

> *Now the overseer must be above reproach...*
>   *1 Timothy 3:2*
>
> *Sincere...*   *1 Timothy 3:8*
>
> *Since an overseer is entrusted with God's work, he*
> *must be blameless...*   *Titus 1:7*
>
> *Upright, holy and disciplined.*   *Titus 1:8*

Hmmm. A tall order. *"Above reproach... blameless... upright... holy..."* When I hear words like that, I immediately become overwhelmed with guilt—and I want to run and hide somewhere!

But don't be confused. **Blameless** doesn't mean **perfect**. There has been only one perfect human being, and I can assure you it ain't me! (It probably ain't you either!)

Being "blameless" or "above reproach" simply means that you are not hiding anything that someone would be able to criticise you about. Being "blameless" or "above reproach" simply means that you acknowledge where you are failing, and you're working hard at dealing with it. Being "blameless" or "above reproach" means that you will go out of your way to not only do what is right, but also to make sure that what you're doing can't be misinterpreted as something wrong. As soon as you start hiding something, or pretending that you are better than you really are, or putting on a leadership front that is simply not honest, then you are no longer "blameless"; you are no longer "above reproach".

When one of our female high-school students says: *"Tim—can I talk personally and privately with you?"*, my answer is: *"Sure—but let's just involve that female leader over there and then the three of us can chat"*.

What's the problem in my chatting personally and privately with a female teenager by myself? Possibly nothing! Let's imagine that **neither** of us has any impure motive for wanting to spend personal and private time together. Even if that were true, here's the problem: How could it be *interpreted* by anyone who was watching? Even if I have nothing impure on my mind, am I placing myself in a position where I could be accused of doing the wrong thing—and have no defence? If anyone wanted to attack our youth ministry, would they be able to say: *"That Tim Hawkins—I don't trust him—I know for a fact that he takes teenage girls away by themselves. Who knows what they get up to?"*

By involving a female leader so that it is a three-way conversation I am making a decision which is "above reproach". **I** am protected if the girl in question makes accusations about me. **The girl** is protected in case my motives are not entirely pure. And **our ministry** is protected by not opening ourselves to the criticism of those who want to destroy us.

These are three questions that you can ask yourself about any decision which is in the area of being "above reproach".

a) Does it protect our leaders against false accusation?

b) Does it protect our young people?

c) Does it protect the good name of our ministry?

There are many other instances where leaders need to take decisions that are "above reproach". This sometimes means placing on ourselves a standard that is higher and tighter than the Bible says. We go "the extra mile" to remove any **hint** of accusation that might be levelled against us.

One of our guidelines for our leaders is that no leader should be romantically linked with a group member. That is, we don't want our adult leaders to "date" high-school students.

This is not a **biblical** standard in itself. The Bible says nothing about this issue. And it gets complicated when some of our leaders are only in their first year out of high school (aged 19), and they might well be attracted to a student in our Year 12 community (say, aged 17 or 18).

But it is simply "not appropriate" for one of our adult leaders to be dating one of our teenagers. You would never allow a young teacher at a school to date one of the senior students! We want parents to send their high-school students to our youth ministry with the assurance that they are not just "date bait" for our young leaders! It is a decision to be "above reproach" which sets the guideline that our leaders should not date our students.

In Appendix Two on page 297, you will find our "Code of Conduct" to help our leaders stay "above reproach". It is not meant to be a legal straightjacket—it is not meant to create a culture where we are ruled by endless laws. We want to be a leadership community who are governed by grace and forgiveness. But take a look at our guidelines, and see how this helps us to maintain a biblical standard.

Let me tell you some good news about being "above reproach". **No matter what you have done, you can <u>always</u> make an "above reproach" decision.** That's right—there is never a time when you cannot take a step towards becoming "blameless". To be "above reproach" simply means that you are not hiding anything, and that you are dealing with any area where you have gone wrong.

One of our young male leaders came to see me. He told me that he was attracted to one of our female high-school students, and that during the school holiday break, they had spent some personal time together, and grown a little too close.

Just press the pause button for a moment...

By coming and disclosing this to me, he had taken an "above reproach" decision. That is, he wasn't hiding anything—he was being open and honest about where he was at. Even if he had allowed himself to be drawn too close to this particular girl, he was now doing the right thing by coming and telling me about this.

As we chatted, we looked at what his options were. One possibility was that he would pursue a relationship with this girl, and step aside from our leadership team as a result. **This would also have been an "above reproach" decision.** That is, nothing hidden. No secret agenda. No mixed motives. A straight-out decision of integrity.

He did not want to go down that path. He decided that he wanted to remain committed to our youth ministry team, which meant he would withdraw from this relationship with this girl immediately.

That was also an "above reproach" decision.

We cried together. We prayed together. We reached a decision of integrity. There were no black marks against his name. He was now a leader who was back to being "above reproach". If anyone else ever came to me to accuse this leader over this particular incident, I would now be able to say: *"Yes, he's already come to me and told me everything. He has taken a decision of integrity. He is now "above reproach."*

There is the world of difference between this situation and where the **opposite** occurs. That is where a leader has stepped over the line, but they keep it to themselves—they continue in an inappropriate relationship—someone else tells me about it—the leader involved denies it… you can imagine the mess that results from this! The leader is open to attack, our ministry is open to attack, and somewhere in the middle of all this, one of our precious teenagers is hurt.

We once had a female leader in our team. Bright, encouraging—real leadership material. She was in her young twenties, and was surely one of our leading lights.

We cheered for her when she became engaged to one of our other young leaders.

A couple of incidents occurred which disturbed me. One afternoon, when I went down to our youth centre (which was closed at the time), I found this female leader there with one of our 16-year-old boys. She explained that they needed to talk. I pointed out that she should not be alone with a student of the opposite sex. She said she was sorry. I thought the issue was over.

Some time later, there was a big Christian festival in our city at a huge camping area, where everyone camped in tents. A group from our church attended. I heard stories coming back that this same female leader had ended up sleeping next to another 16-year-old boy in his tent. When I caught up with her, she explained that in the middle of the night, her tent was torn down by the strong wind, and she had nowhere to sleep, and that this particular boy had offered his help—which meant sharing his tent with her. I cautioned her that she was stepping way outside our guidelines and asked her whether anything was "going on". She told me that it was just an innocent mistake and she promised me she would be more careful. Maybe I was naïve, but I believed her.

A little later I heard reports that she had been sitting alone in a park with this same 16-year-old boy. I confronted her with this. She denied it. I was not satisfied, so I caught up with the boy concerned. He told me everything. The two of them were in a romantic relationship, and had been for some time. Yes, he knew she was engaged to someone else, but, well, she was a **leader**, so he thought everything must be okay.

I caught up with the leader one more time. When I confronted her with the conversation I had had with the boy, she eventually confessed. She told me that she had started making a play for him **on the night of her engagement party**. She had been involved in a cover-up since then.

There were no decisions of integrity in this case. She was never in a situation where she was "above reproach". She was doing the wrong thing. She was covering it up. She was pleading her innocence the whole time. She was not truthful in any of our dealings.

She is no longer on our leadership team. She broke off her engagement. Her brief fling with the 16-year-old boy ended. There were no good endings in this story.

This incident failed each of the questions I suggested before:

a) Did it protect our leaders against false accusation?

b) Did it protect our young people?

c) Did it protect the good name of our ministry?

The sad answer in each case was "no".

No wonder the Bible says:

> *They must first be tested; and then if there is nothing against them, let them serve as deacons.*
>
> *1 Timothy 3:10*

If you're going to be a leader who is "above reproach", then you need to check carefully in your life whether there is anything that you are hiding. None of the other qualities of a leader will make sense if you don't work on this one. Remember, whatever you have done, whatever has happened, **you can always still make a decision to be "above reproach"**. We have a God who loves to see us coming back to him. We have a God who loves to restore us.

5. It's a good thing to be a leader!

In the next chapter we will look at eight ways that God's word gives you to help you stay "above reproach" as a leader. But just before we get there, let's back off for a moment.

Right now you might be thinking: *"I can't keep this standard! It's too hard for me! I want to get out of here!"* Yes, biblical leadership is at a high standard—but God wants us to hang in there and be the very best that we are able to be.

Let me show you two encouragements which sit right in the centre of these lists of leadership qualities.

> *Here is a trustworthy saying: If anyone sets his heart on being an overseer, he desires a noble task.*
> **1 Timothy 3:1**

It is a good thing to be a leader. It is a good thing to **want** to be a leader. It's a noble task. It's a great task. It's a task worth doing. There may be cost involved. There may be a change in lifestyle needed. There might be aspects of your walk with Jesus that aren't the way that they should be. **But it is worth doing.** And it is worth doing well.

> *Those who have served well gain an excellent standing and great assurance in their faith in Christ Jesus.*   **1 Timothy 3:13**

In all my years as a youth leader, I have grown so much by being a youth leader. I sometimes think to myself: *"I know I'm growing every time I lead young people. I just hope that they're growing as well!"* Every time I interact with a young person, I learn something. Every time I teach them something, I learn something myself.

My faith is so much stronger simply because I've hung in there on the roller-coaster of youth leadership. So stick with it. You might have some crazy ups and downs—but I can assure you that you're in for the ride of your life!

If we investigate the rest of the four biblical lists for leaders (see previous chapter), then we'll discover some great checkpoints to help you stay "above reproach" in everything that you do. Remember, God is a God of grace and forgiveness, and he wants the absolute best for you. These checkpoints in the Bible are there to help you to achieve your absolute best, to impact others in the most effective way, and to enjoy the journey of leadership that God has placed before you.

Chapter 13

Eight checkpoints for a biblical leader

1. Check your growth

If you are a leader—if you are giving out to others—then it really matters that you make sure you keep growing strongly as a Christian. If you're giving out without taking in, then you'll run dry really quickly.

One of our guidelines for our leaders is that they need to be growing in one of our small Bible-study groups. Many of our leaders are youngish in their faith, and we want to make sure that we're looking after them! Sometimes we will discover that one of our leaders has "slipped through the cracks", and isn't being looked after in a small group. Often, when we catch up, they will say something like: *"Time's a bit of a pressure at the moment. I don't think I have the time to lead in the youth ministry **and** be in a small Bible-study group."* This is perfectly understandable. What we would normally say back to them is: *"Well, why don't you take a break from your youth ministry, so that you can re-establish your growth in a small group?"*

Maintaining your personal spiritual growth while you are a leader **really matters**.

Here are three ways to help you stay on track:

a) Don't rush ahead of your spiritual maturity

He must not be a recent convert, or he may become conceited and fall under the same judgment as the devil.   *1 Timothy 3:6*

This has been discussed in Chapter 8, Section 2—The character tree. If you're only a very young Christian and you've been given a ministry with lots of responsibility, then you might need to go back to your pastor, and arrange a bit of a "breather" so that you can put some solid work into your own growth. Similarly, if you're recruiting others to your leadership team, don't ask people who have only just started to follow Jesus. If someone's ministry is racing ahead of their own spiritual growth, then they are heading for disaster.

Karen was a vibrant young student. A great high-schooler who had recently come to Christ. And God had blessed her with a beautiful voice. We were very tempted to give her a mike and ask her to do the many solos that we needed in our youth praise and music.

But we didn't. We held her in the vocal group, and trained her along with a whole stack of other high-schoolers. We made sure she was being developed as a disciple in one of our "D-Teams". Our ministry was to prepare her as a **disciple** first, before placing her in a "spotlight" ministry. We wanted to make sure that her ministry wasn't rushing ahead of her spiritual maturity. We didn't want her to *"become conceited and fall under the same judgment as the devil"*.

Karen grew strongly as a disciple. Now as an adult she has an **awesome** ministry in our creative arts team. She still has that same beautiful voice—but now as she leads our congregation, she sings with the depth of a young woman who loves Jesus deeply and is continuing to grow strongly.

b) Hold firmly to God's word

They must keep hold of the deep truths of the faith with a clear conscience. **1 Timothy 3:9**

He must hold firmly to the trustworthy message as it has been taught. **Titus 1:9**

Once you've started on your journey as a Christian, **hang on in there**! If you want to be an awesome leader, then you need to hold firmly to everything you have been taught from God's word.

Do you know what it means to "hold firmly"?

Imagine you're climbing a cliff face—and you're attempting to gain a foothold on the rock—and to help you do it you have reached out with your hands and grabbed on to a small branch that is jutting out from the cliff. Your whole weight is being supported by this branch. Your life depends on how firmly you hang on. Relax your grip for just one moment and your life is on the line.

The biblical leader is called to *"hold firmly to the trustworthy message"* in the same way. Hang on firmly to everything you have been taught from God's word. Don't stray away for even a moment. Your life depends on this!

c) Flee from sin

Flee the evil desires of youth, and pursue righteousness, faith, love and peace, along with those who call on the Lord out of a pure heart.

2 Timothy 2:22

"Yeah, yeah—I know—if I'm going to be a good leader, I need to stay away from sin."

That's not what the passage says. God's word doesn't just tell leaders to "stay away" from sin. Read it again. 2 Timothy 2:22 says, "**Flee**"! Run away from it! Get as far away as possible! Go in the completely opposite direction!

As a leader, I need to be reminded of this. Sometimes, in my effort to avoid sin, I like to keep it around where I can still see it. You know, close enough so I'm never that far away from it. I'm not going to **do** the sin, mind you, but I just want to stay close enough so I can watch it from a distance.

This is dangerous stuff. A leader needs to work hard to keep their life on track with what God's word says. If you keep sin close at hand, you will eventually go back to it in a moment of weakness.

Do you want to be a leader that holds to a biblical standard? Then flee from anything which would distract you from being a faithful disciple.

Is there anything lurking around in your life at the moment that you need to flee from?

2. Check your family relationships

When we check the biblical lists for leaders, we find some very strange words. Qualities that rarely appear in any modern-day books about leadership!

The overseer must be ... the husband of but one wife.
1 Timothy 3:2

An elder must be ... the husband of but one wife, a man whose children believe and are not open to the charge of being wild and disobedient. **Titus 1:6**

> *In the same way, their wives are to be women worthy*
> *of respect, not malicious talkers but temperate*
> *and trustworthy in everything. A deacon must be*
> *the husband of but one wife and must manage his*
> *children and his household well.*   **1 Timothy 3:11-12**

Strange words indeed! One of God's standards for leadership is to make sure your spouse and your children are **also** growing in Christian maturity! How can this be? How could the personal life of someone's spouse or children ever have a bearing on their ability to be a leader in God's church?

The Bible has the simple answer:

> *He must manage his own family well and see that*
> *his children obey him with proper respect. (If anyone*
> *does not know how to manage his own family, how*
> *can he take care of God's church?)*   **1 Timothy 3:4-5**

That's it! Simple, really. How can someone claim that they are a leader in God's family, when they can't even exercise leadership in their own family?

As far as God is concerned, leadership is a **total** issue. You don't become a leader *"just when you're at church"*, any more than you become loving *"just when you're at church"*, or humble *"just when you're at church"*. You can't claim to bring a ministry to the family of God when you can't even be bothered having a ministry to your family at home!

So, if you want to check how you're going as a Christian leader, then check how you're going in your relationships at home.

"What about single leaders?"

I'm glad you asked! There's nothing that says Christian leaders have to be married. The Bible is merely saying: *"If you are married, then make sure you only have one wife (or one husband, as the case may be!)"*

If you still live at home with your parents, then apply the same principle to your relationship with your parents. Do you honour and respect them the same way that the Bible says? If at church you are teaching young people how to respect rightful authority, do you model it in the way you treat your parents?

If you're a young leader with a passion to fix up the mess in the world, have you started by fixing up the mess in your bedroom?

Everything that is true about your Christian character will be modelled by how you act at home!

3. Check your reputation

Listen to these words from the biblical lists:

> *The overseer must be ... respectable.*   ***1 Timothy 3:2***

> *Deacons, likewise, are to be men worthy of respect.*
> ***1 Timothy 3:8***

> *He must also have a good reputation with outsiders, so that he will not fall into disgrace and into the devil's trap.*   ***1 Timothy 3:7***

How you are viewed by others—your reputation—really matters if you want to be a biblical leader. If people don't respect you—if you don't have a good reputation with others—then it is unlikely they will ever let you have a good ministry with them.

But how can I control what others think about me?

Well, you can't. Sometimes people will have the wrong idea of what you're like. Even Jesus was misunderstood. At various times, he was accused of being a drunkard, a womaniser, and a political revolutionary!

Maybe you're a very honest person, but because others have misunderstood you, or listened to rumours, then they might believe you are basically dishonest. That is, your character is basically **good**, but your reputation is basically **bad**.

It can work the other way as well. Perhaps you present yourself at church as being squeaky clean with a high moral standard. But maybe at home you are addicted to watching pornography on internet sites. That is, your character is basically **bad**, but your reputation is basically **good**.

It might just be that other people have the wrong idea about you. You can't **change** what they think, but you can certainly influence what they think. Check out the three principles below.

a) Your character is more important than your reputation

That's exactly what Jesus said when he challenged the religious leaders of his day.

> *Woe to you, teachers of the law and Pharisees, you hypocrites! You are like whitewashed tombs, which look beautiful on the outside but on the inside are full of dead men's bones and everything unclean. In the same way, on the outside you appear to people as righteous but on the inside you are full of hypocrisy and wickedness.* **Matthew 23:27-28**

Jesus attacked the religious leaders of his day because their **reputation** looked great on the outside, but their **character** was rotten on the inside.

Your character is more important than your reputation.

Your reputation is what other people **THINK** you're like.

Your character is what you're **REALLY** like.

Your reputation is what is seen on the **outside**.

Your character is what is real on the **inside**.

b) To change your reputation, work on your character
What was Jesus' advice to the religious leaders of the day?

> *Woe to you, teachers of the law and Pharisees, you hypocrites! You clean the outside of the cup and dish, but inside they are full of greed and self-indulgence. Blind Pharisee! First clean the inside of the cup and dish, and then the outside also will be clean.*
> **Matthew 23:25-26**

Jesus says:

> *"You spend so much time making sure that you look squeaky clean on the **outside**! What you need to do is clean up your act on the **inside**—and then the outside will be clean as well!"*

If your reputation ain't what it should be, start the change from the inside out! Start working on your character! Allow God to change your heart on the inside, and you will see fantastic and awesome changes happen on the outside.

c) What's on the inside will always come out

If you are opening your heart to the work of God's Holy Spirit, then how you live on the outside will change. If you're letting God change and re-shape what you are like deep inside, then how others view you on the outside **will change**. If you are growing a character that is becoming more and more like Jesus himself, your reputation among others **will change**.

Just check that what is on the inside is what you want to come out!

4. Check your drinking habits

Okay—okay—what's going on here? We're talking about being a leader in God's church! What do you mean "Check your drinking habits"?

It's interesting. Avoiding drunkenness is specifically mentioned in three of the four lists.

> *The overseer must be ... not given to drunkenness.*
> **1 Timothy 3:3**

> *An overseer ... must be ... not given to drunkenness.*
> **Titus 1:7**

> *Deacons, likewise, are to be men ... not indulging in much wine.*   **1 Timothy 3:8**

Okay, there are many failings that Christian leaders can fall into? Why single out drunkenness?

a) The Bible has nothing against alcohol...

Alcohol is often spoken about as a symbol of God's great blessing (Proverbs 3:9-10, Psalm 104:14-15, Joel 3:17-18). Even Jesus himself drank (Luke 7:33-34) and for his first miracle, he provided wine at a friend's wedding! (John 2:1-11).

b) But it's a question of control

While the Bible never condemns alcohol, there is strong condemnation for getting drunk!

> *Do not get drunk on wine, which leads to debauchery.*
> *Instead, be filled with the Spirit.*   **Ephesians 5:18**

It's really a question of what controls you. God wants you to be controlled by his Holy Spirit. He wants you to be **filled** with his Spirit. He doesn't want anything else to control you. As soon as alcohol is starting to have an effect on the sort of person you are, it is starting to exercise some control. Ephesians 5:18 is suggesting that the more you allow alcohol to control you, the less open you are to God's Spirit controlling you.

c) Drunkenness gets in the way of leadership

Imagine a situation where one of God's leaders is affected by alcohol when he is receiving a message from God! Imagine a Christian leader being drunk at the same time he is making ministry decisions which will affect the lives of others!

Can you believe that is the very situation that is tackled by Isaiah as he reveals his prophecy?

> *Priests and prophets stagger from beer and are*
> *befuddled with wine; they reel from beer, they stagger*
> *when seeing visions, they stumble when rendering*
> *decisions. All the tables are covered with vomit and*
> *there is not a spot without filth.*   **Isaiah 28:7-8**

Leadership and drunkenness cannot go together. Probably drunkenness is no worse than any other sin, but it is an incredibly **public** sin! Everyone knows about it! Everyone loves to talk about it! If leaders are to guard their reputation, drunkenness can have no part in their lives.

5. Check your temper

Your temper is a funny thing—just when you think you have it totally under control, something powerful sneaks out and catches you unaware.

Look at what the biblical lists have to say about the "temper" of a Christian leader:

> *Temperate, self-controlled … not violent but gentle.*
> **1 Timothy 3:2-3**

> *Not overbearing, not quick-tempered, not violent …*
> *self-controlled."* **Titus 1:7-8**

I think I am a very even-tempered person. I don't flare up quickly. When things go wrong, I can usually remain pretty calm and stay on top of my emotions.

I have some friends who are completely different. They are "over the top" in every way! When something funny happens—they laugh uproariously loud and long. When their football team wins—they're pumped for days! When they get cut off in traffic—man—they're as mad as hell and sit hard on the horn to let the other guy know what a goose he is!

Sometimes we think it's only the second sort of person that has a problem with temper. But we "quiet" ones also need to be on our guard to make sure we "check our temper".

Many years ago, we ran a youth-outreach programme at our church. We had an old church hall, and the neighbourhood kids would rock up while we attempted to introduce them to Jesus. It was pretty hard going, with some pretty difficult kids. Most of our leaders were at the end of their rope by the time the evening finished.

I had a van, and I would give a lift to many of the kids so they would get home safely. There was one particular night, where I was pretty worn out. It was the end of the programme, and I had a van full of kids waiting to leave. This 14-year-old girl raced over **and stole my car keys**! She raced off with my keys—leaving me and my whole van-full stranded, with a silly "tee-hee-hee" in her voice that said, *"You just try and catch me!"*

I was so mad! How **dare** she take my keys! Here I am, right in the middle of trying to help these kids by taking them home (many of them had curfews), we were running late—and this 14-year-old girl stops the whole procedure by taking my keys!

I chased after her. She raced into our church hall and slammed the door behind her. She was on the inside holding the door shut—I was on the outside trying to push my way in. I was a little bigger and stronger than she was, so slowly I inched the door opened. She resisted with all her might, but slowly I was conquering her. I pushed the door open enough so she was pinned behind it against the brick wall. I knew she was stuck behind the door—being pinned against the wall—**and I kept pushing**! I was as mad as hell and I wanted to hurt her.

One of my leaders rushed in and exclaimed: *"Tim—what are you doing?"* I realised that I was crushing this poor girl behind the door, and my only motive was revenge. My temper had got the better of me. I backed off. I apologised. I had a lot of explaining to do.

No wonder the Bible says to leaders "check your temper". Be aware of your danger points. Understand what pushes your buttons. Make yourself accountable to others in your leadership team so that they can help stop you from going over the edge.

Good leadership can be undermined by an uncontrolled temper.

6. Check your words

Something came over me when I was a young leader, fresh out of Bible college. **I knew I was right!** (And, by implication, I knew most others were wrong!) I was right about my understanding of the Bible (because I knew more theology than anyone else), I was right about my ministry strategy (after all, I had been to Bible college), and I was right about getting rid of all the traditional ways of doing ministry (because I was more in tune with today's world than anyone else).

I remember being a cabin leader on a week-long youth camp. The studies for the week were based around "The four spiritual laws". This was the way we were going to present the gospel to the kids. I can remember getting into an argument with the camp director, and trying to show why theologically "The four spiritual laws" weren't the best way to present the gospel, and how they were biblically unsound (Ouch!).

It was a strange disease that overtook me. It was the "I'm-a-new-leader-and-I've-had-some-leadership-training" syndrome. A dangerous breed indeed!

Listen to God's word:

> *Don't have anything to do with foolish and stupid arguments, because you know they produce quarrels. And the Lord's servant must not quarrel."*
> **2 Timothy 2:23-24** *(see also 1 Timothy 3:3)*

Hmmm. So much for getting into arguments because I knew I was right! Mind you—you might just need to take a stand for the truth, and there may be times that you will tackle issues because others have strayed away from the clear teaching of God's word. But there are so many issues where there is no **need** to start a quarrel. Okay—so someone's interpretation of the Bible doesn't conform exactly to my well-thought-out theological stance. **Big deal!** Maybe my theological viewpoint is imperfect (now—there's a thought!). Perhaps **I** have something still to learn? (Is it possible?) Do I want to win this argument to uphold God's honour—or my own honour?

I have known young leaders, good leaders with fire in their bellies, who have taken on every issue at the church they work for. Nothing is good enough. Everyone is making errors. Everything must be changed.

Do you want to check how you're going at being a biblical leader? Then take note: *"The Lord's servant must not quarrel"*.

Check your words!

7. Check your wallet

Okay—now we're getting down to the serious stuff! If you want to check how you're going with your attitude to **leadership**, then the Bible says you should check how you're going with your attitude to **money**. Three of the four lists mention it.

> *The overseer must be … not a lover of money.*
> **1 Timothy 3:3**

> *Deacons, likewise, are to be … not pursuing dishonest gain.* **1 Timothy 3:8**

> *An overseer … must be … not pursuing dishonest gain.* **Titus 1:7**

There is nothing wrong with money in itself. The Bible is clear that it is the **love** of money that is the problem (1 Timothy 6:10).

I could never work this one out. In my church culture, ministers were always paid poorly. And if you went and preached at another church or ministry organisation, you were lucky to get petrol money. How could any Christian leader be *"a lover of money"* or *"pursuing dishonest gain"*?

Some of my friends have opened my eyes on this one. I hear that in certain circles, some leaders pick and choose which outside ministries they will speak at based on how large the "love offering" (voluntary donation for the speaker) might be at the end of it!

Think of it this way:

> *Be shepherds of God's flock that is under your care, serving as overseers—not because you must, but because you are willing, as God wants you to be; not greedy for money, but eager to serve.* **1 Peter 5:2**

The **opposite** of being "eager to serve" is to be "greedy for money". And the one thing that God wants of every Christian leader is that they will be "eager to serve".

You can approach leadership in two ways. You're either in it for God and his people, or you're in it for yourself. You're either in ministry for what you can give to others, or what you can gain for yourself. And if you're looking for your own gain—there's more than money on offer here! Perhaps you're after status... or recognition... or power... or glory... or gratification... or brownie-points in God's kingdom... or a promotion?

What is your attitude to your money and your possessions? A leader is called upon to be generous—a faithful steward of what God has placed before them. A Christian leader will want to honour God with his money and his possessions. A Christian leader will want to be the most generous person in his congregation (you can't ask people to give at a level that is higher than you are prepared to give yourself!).

Do you want to check how you're going at being a biblical leader? Then check your wallet! Check how you're going with your attitude to your money and possessions.

> *For where your treasure is, there your heart will be also.* **Matthew 6:21**

8. Check your attitude

One of the great things about God's standards for leaders is that he treats us as whole people. That is, there isn't a set of standards for when we're being leaders, and then a different set while we're having time off. Each one of us is a **whole** person, and God calls us to be faithful to him **the whole time**.

So whether you're in leadership mode or not, one of the best ways to stay accountable to God's standard is to check out your attitude—on everything!

Here are four key attitude-checks for you:

a) Hospitable
See 1 Timothy 3:2; Titus 1:8.

The essence of being "hospitable" is that you gladly share what you have with others. The original meaning of course, is that you share your home with others—even with strangers! In Jesus' time, where people had to walk on their journeys for days to get to the next village, it was important that people opened their homes to travellers. If they didn't, they were placing these weary travellers in extreme danger! (This wonderful aspect of hospitality still sometimes occurs in the remote Australian outback!)

In our days of modern, crowded cities, with houses with security grills over every window and door, and with con-men and thieves looking for every opportunity of taking advantage of some hapless householder, we probably need to be more careful in the literal interpretation of "opening your home to strangers"! However the **principle** still applies—a leader should be generous with their own possessions.

There are many youth leaders who open their house regularly to the youth of their church. This sends a strong message that **people** are more important than our **possessions**. There is, of course, always a risk involved!

Karen and I had just built a new house. Everything brand new. Clean. Undamaged. We invited all our Year 12 students to come down for supper one evening after church. About

50 arrived, and we welcomed this rambling multitude into our new surroundings.

Everything was going fine until one of these hefty young men sat down on one of our coffee tables. The problem was that this table was primarily designed for supporting reasonably lightweight cups of coffee—rather than the somewhat bulky and very adult-sized body of an emerging young man.

The result? A total collapse of the aforementioned coffee table… and the young man… and the cups of coffee on it! The young man recovered, which is more than can be said for the cups of coffee or the table itself (or the carpet!).

There is often a price to pay for hospitality!

The essence of being hospitable is: **People are more important than your possessions**.

Maybe you don't have a house that you can share. Perhaps it's your car. One of the occupational hazards of being a youth leader is giving endless lifts to teenagers who have no other way of getting around. While you might have standards of what is and isn't acceptable conduct in your car, whenever you allow someone else into your car, you are accepting the possibility that they might just trash it a little. (Certainly the amount of rubbish left in my car is in direct proportion to the number of young people I have given a lift to!)

Maybe it's your iPod that you need to be hospitable with. Or your electric guitar. Or your money. Yes, there are always risks involved in being hospitable. And yes, you need to be wise in your stewardship of your possessions.

But check it out. Does your attitude to what you own show that people matter more to you than your possessions? That is a mark of being hospitable. That is a mark of being a biblical leader.

b) Kind
See 2 Timothy 2:24.

Somewhere along the line, the idea of being "kind" got hijacked. This good, strong, active, biblical word somehow got replaced with the weak, generic and "oh-so-pleasant" word "nice". You know, "nice", as in "Have a nice day". "Nice", as in "being appealing… pleasing… polite".

Maybe there's nothing wrong with "nice", but don't confuse it with "kind". Even a bad leader can be "nice". But the biblical leader is always called upon to be "kind".

God wasn't just "nice" to us. He wasn't just pleasant—or pleasing—or polite. He was "kind". That is, he had genuine compassion for us. His heart was moved to sorrow for us. He lavished his love upon us. He does for us things that we simply do not deserve. God is actively and boldly kind in the way he deals with us.

One of the marks of a biblical leader is that he is kind. You need to be kind in the same way God has been kind to us.

What did it mean for God to be kind to us?

> *But when the kindness and love of God our Saviour appeared, he saved us, not because of righteous things we had done, but because of his mercy. He saved us through the washing of rebirth and renewal by the Holy Spirit, whom he poured out on us generously through Jesus Christ our Saviour, so that,*

> *having been justified by his grace, we might become*
> *heirs having the hope of eternal life.*   ***Titus 3:4-7***

To be kind to us, God lavished his love upon us even to the point of sacrificing his own Son. This is not just being "nice". This is being "kind". And **that** is what a Christian leader is called to be!

c) Not resentful
See 2 Timothy 2:24.

It's not hard to be resentful in youth ministry. You find yourself working hard—darn hard. You put in stacks of effort, sometimes seeing very little return and not much appreciation. And maybe this thought comes streaming through your head: *"Why do I bother? Why do I have to do all this? Why can't someone else put in a bit of effort for a change?"*

Familiar words? I have exclaimed them (quietly!) often!

While I was at Bible college, I was a student-minister on the weekends at one of the churches in Sydney. I had worked in the youth-ministry area there for about 18 months, and it was now time for me to move on to my next church—for further training in different areas. The congregation held a small farewell supper for me after my last church service with them. Very nice.

When it was over, it was time to clean up the hall. And, as it had happened every night for the previous 18 months, there I was with a broom in hand, sweeping the whole hall out. As a faithful, submissive servant? No way! I was growling within myself: *"How come I have to clean up after my own farewell?"* (I guess it had nothing to do with my own lack of leadership skills!)

Feeling resentful is a sure sign that something else is not working in your Christian life. If you find you're resenting the effort that leadership takes, then call "time out". Deal with the inner issues, so that you might return to your leadership full of enthusiasm to serve others.

d) Loves what is good
See Titus 1:8

One of the hallmarks of being a biblical leader is that you love what is good.

"Of course I love what is good! I'm a Christian leader!"

Fair enough. Do you really love it when something good **happens to another person** (and not to you)? Do you really love it when something good is **done by another person** and not by you? Do you really love it when you do something really good and **someone else gets the credit**?

A Christian leader is someone who **loves what is good**, irrespective of who gets the credit.

Does that describe you? One of the great attributes of a Christian leader is that they love what is good.

God has given us these check-points so that we can be biblical leaders of a high standard. He has also provided overwhelming forgiveness when we fail his standards and walk away from him. But he wants you to succeed—and these checkpoints are here to help you.

God has called us to a high standard. He has given us his Spirit that we might walk in his ways. Let's be high-integrity leaders in his service, so that we truly can be described as being "above reproach".

SECTION 3

Grow your leadership skills

Chapter 14

You are a Bible teacher

One of the huge privileges of being a biblical leader is that you get to teach God's word to others. Perhaps you will preach to hundreds... or thousands. Maybe you will lead a small Bible-study group. Or even teach God's word one-on-one in an individual discipling relationship.

But whatever it is, you cannot escape the fact that the main way you will help young people to change their life, is by helping them to apply God's word to their life.

So, if you're going to teach the Bible, how do you make sure that you do it correctly? How do you ensure that the message you proclaim is in fact what God wants you to say? And how can you be effective in communicating powerfully?

This is a chapter on "how to". That is, if you have to teach the Bible to others, how do you go about doing it so that your message is true, bold and effective?

1. Before you begin...
Here are some important questions to ask yourself!

a) Is the Bible working in your life?
It's no use trying to teach others the Bible unless you first make sure that it is working in your own life!

> *You, then, who teach others, do you not teach yourself? You who preach against stealing, do you steal? You who say that people should not commit adultery, do you commit adultery? You who abhor idols, do you rob temples? You who brag about the law, do you dishonour God by breaking the law?*
>
> **Romans 2:21-23**

So check it out!

Are you regularly reading the Bible—by yourself, and with others?

When you read the Bible, do you hear God speaking to you?

When God speaks to you, do you respond by obeying him?

b) Do you want God's help?

If it is God's message that we are wanting to communicate, then we'd better ask for his help!

As a young leader, I remember preparing a Bible study on "prayer". I was going to present this at the youth group on Sunday, and I wanted to make sure that it would be impactful. I was working hard on it—researching what the Bible said, looking for practical illustrations, designing exercises to help people to be real in their prayers—and then a horrible thought dawned on me. **I hadn't prayed about it!** How embarrassing! I was preparing a Bible study on prayer, and I hadn't even bothered doing the very thing that I was planning to teach others—pray!

Prayer is not an interruption to your hard work of preparation. It is the very heart and soul of your message.

If you're going to present God's word to others, then remember the words of Jesus:

Apart from me you can do nothing. **John 15:5**

c). Do you understand God and where he is "at"?

If you're teaching about God, then you need to know him well! It's not enough to simply know **about** him. You need to know him. Be intimate with him. Worship him. Live for him. You are about to introduce others to him. Make sure you know him well enough to introduce him well!

d) Do you understand your audience and where they are "at"?

As well as knowing God, you also need to know the world that your listeners are in. You need to understand what it is like to walk in their shoes—and how the word of God will impact and change their lives.

Ask these four basic questions:

* *What is going on in their world?*

* *What is their level of understanding?*

* *What is their point of need and interest?*

* *What is the entry point for God's word into their world?*

Many Bible studies and sermons fail at this point. The leader simply **assumes** that their listeners think the same as they do, live in the same world, and face the same issues. This is rarely true. Especially in youth ministry!

e) What is your aim?

These important questions are often missed:

Why am I taking this Bible study (or sermon)?

What am I really hoping will be achieved?

When it is all over, what is the one result that I want people to walk away with?

You need to have this end result in mind. Everything you do in your Bible study or sermon needs to lead to this point. If you get to the end of it all, and someone were to ask, *"So what?"*—would the answer be obvious?

You need to know your aim so you know where to head. Remember: *"if you aim at nothing, then you're sure to hit it!"*

2. The four parts of your presentation

Once you've worked through these preliminary steps, I want to suggest that every good sermon or Bible study has four major sections. Avoid any of these steps at your own peril! And, yes, for easy memory—they all rhyme!

a) "The hook"

The "hook" is the way you will open your presentation so that you engage the minds and hearts of your hearers. In any sermon or Bible study, you have about thirty seconds to convince people that you are worth listening to, and that they should be interested in where you're heading.

So think carefully about your opening. Write it down, and **do not vary it**. Think through some questions like these:

How will you grab your audience's attention **in your first sentence**?

What is your audience's point of need or interest?

What will start them thinking about the issue you want to present?

How can you show your audience that you are in tune with where they are at?

If I am preparing a sermon, I will often put at least an hour's preparation into these vital opening five minutes. **Because if you don't get your audience on board with where you're heading, then it doesn't matter how good the rest of your Bible teaching is!**

It's like driving a train. You, the Bible teacher, are like the train driver. Your job is to pick up your passengers at the station, and deliver them to your destination. You need to know your destination—that is your aim. You need to know the best way to get there—that is your Bible teaching. But you also need to know how to get your passengers on the train—that is your hook.

You might have the best Bible study or sermon in the world. You might have the greatest destination planned for your students. You might have the shiniest new train—you might be the best train driver on the planet—**but unless you get your passengers off the platform—and WANTING to travel on your train—then you are going for a journey ALL BY YOURSELF.**

And believe me, I've heard many sermons—and sat through many Bible studies—where the leader was on a journey "all by themselves"!

Take the time to get people on board with you. They might not realise that they need to go to your destination—they might not like your particular train—they might not even trust your driving. You might need to convince them that the journey is going to be worthwhile!

Here are some clues as to how to have an effective "hook".

i. Don't open with a joke

Most jokes aren't all that funny. You need to be very careful about starting with a joke **because it might fall flat**! And if your audience doesn't like your opening line, it might be very hard work to get them back on board!

ii. Use humour

This might sound like an odd thing to say now that I have warned you not to open with a joke. But use lots of humour—because humour has a way of disarming even the most hostile audience.

How do you use humour without telling jokes?

A joke is a "setup"—where there is an artificial story which relies on a punchline. *"There was an Englishman, an American and an Australian…"*; *"There was a travelling salesman who was out in the country, so he pulls into a farmhouse to stay the night…"* There are thousands more like this, but you get the general idea.

But the best humour doesn't rely on jokes! The **best** humour simply describes everyday life, and draws out the funny side of it. Watch some stand-up comedians on TV, and you'll probably notice that most of them simply relate everyday incidences—and draw out the funny side of them. Watch them—and learn from them. *(And while you're getting started—borrow their material!)*

Clifford Warne, an Australian storyteller who wrote *"How to hold an audience without a rope"*, once described the difference this way: *"A comic is a person who says funny things; a comedian is a person who says things funny"*. Try and learn the habit of "saying things funny". Use personal incidences that everyone can identify with and draw out the humour in them.

iii. Use personal examples

Your hearers need to know that you are a real person who faces the same issues in life as they do. They need to hear of you successes—and your failures! They love to hear funny stories of how you got things wrong!

iv. Describe their world

The most important thing you need to do in any introduction is to let your hearers know that you understand the world that they live in. You need to describe experiences where they are nodding, saying: *"Yes—my world's like that. That person up the front understands what's going on for me"*. Once you get people nodding in agreement with you, you know you have them on your train—and they're ready to leave on the journey with you.

v. Identify with them emotionally

Somewhere in your first five minutes, you need to identify emotionally with your audience. What do you imagine they're feeling? Are you talking to a group of teenagers who are frustrated by the demands of their parents? Identify with that frustration! Are you talking to young people who might have been used or abused by a sexual partner? Identify with that feeling! You don't have to have felt the same things as your hearers have—and you don't need to know exactly how they feel—you simply need to let them know that it is okay that they have those feelings, and that you understand that things might be a little tough for them at the moment.

Once you have identified emotionally with your hearers, you probably have them on your train, ready to travel with you.

b) "The book"
This is the most important part of your presentation. **What is God's word actually saying to this situation?** You need to do the hard work to get the teaching from the Bible clear. Once you have your passengers on your train, it is "the book"—that is, your clear teaching from the Bible itself—which will keep them on track and ensure they get to the correct destination.

Ask yourself key questions such as:

What biblical material will you be looking at?

What information from the Bible meets the real needs of your audience?

What is God's word actually saying?

This is such an important section of your Bible study or sermon. If you're only going to get one section right, **this is the one to get right**, because if you're not teaching people the same message as the Bible does, **you are not a good Bible teacher**!

This is such an important step—so there are some key details a little later in this chapter.

c) "The look"
Once you have declared what God's word is saying, "the look" is where you explore it with your hearers. In a Bible study, these would be your discussion questions. In a sermon, this is where you start exploring the message

in different situations, and helping people to see the implications of God's message.

Ask key questions such as:

How can you get your audience to discover **for themselves** the truths from the Bible that you want them to learn?

What are the questions that need to be asked so that the Bible answers will make sense?

How can the biblical material change your audience's perspective on what their real needs are and how they will be met?

This section is where you get your hearers **into** God's word to discover its truth for themselves. This is where you start to explore issues which will impact their world. This is where your Bible study or sermon stops being a generic message, which could apply equally to everyone throughout the world, and starts becoming a specific word from God to this particular group of people.

d) "The took"

I can remember when I was a student at Bible college—helping out with youth leadership at a local church. I had just presented a Bible study to our junior-high group. We were doing a series of studies on "Jesus"—and I had just concluded a study which showed that Jesus truly was God. We had looked up the Scriptures—we had heard from the Bible—the proof was indisputable. The study was over. I was feeling good. The young people had been suitably educated.

Just as I was thinking, *"What a jolly good job I've done"*, the associate pastor (who had sat in on the whole thing) then asked a question to the whole group which rung in my ears—and I will never forget it. This is a question which has changed the way I preach and teach up to this very day. His question only had two words in it, but it stays with me every time I open God's word to teach from it.

"So what?"

That was it. *"So what?"* The young people looked nervous—and went strangely silent. All eyes turned to me. I had no idea what to say.

"What do you mean—so what?" (I thought if I asked him to explain himself, I could buy some time to think of a plausible answer.)

He replied: *"So what if Jesus is God? Why does it matter? How does it change my life? Would it make any difference to my faith if he **wasn't** God?"*

I was stunned. I was silent. **I had no idea how to answer his question.** I had left out possibly the most crucial and challenging part of any teaching from the Bible—the application. That is—how is my life meant to change as a result of what I've learned today?

"The took" is what you want your hearers to take away with them. "The took" is where God's word is applied specifically to the lives of each of your hearers. "The took" is where the truth of the Bible starts to be lived out in the lives of everyone who has been impacted by it. "The took" is where ordinary Bible teaching takes on a prophetic edge and is applied chillingly and directly to the very heart of each listener. "The took" is where you ask the profound and life-changing question "So what?"

I must confess I have heard many sermons and sat through many Bible studies where the Bible was faithfully and correctly taught, where biblical truth was presented in an accurate and efficient way, but which left me with absolutely no idea why I needed to hear it or how my life should change as a result! If you go to all the hard work to present the truth of God's word from the Bible, then take the extra effort to make sure you apply it carefully to the life of each of your hearers.

Ask these key questions:

- *What do you want your audience to take away with them?*

- *How does God's word apply directly to their own situation?*

- *How should someone's life change as a result of what they've learned today?*

Some suggestions:

i. Keep it simple
One or two key application points are better than half a dozen. Select the one or two points where you know lives need to change—and emphasise these.

ii. Keep it personal
There is a prophetic touch to good Bible teaching. So don't generalise with "what must we all do?" Individualise it. "What does God want **you** to do?"

iii. Keep it specific

This is where you need to know your hearers. You need to understand the world that they live in. You need to know where they are doing well—and you need to know the sins they are struggling with. The more specific you can be with your application, the more God's word will cut through each person's defences.

So don't just have a general application like: *"We all need to be sexually pure"*. If you know your audience, you can be far more specific with challenges such as: *"Are there websites that you're visiting that you know are dragging you down?" "Are there stories that you're telling—or listening to—that drag sexuality through the gutter" "Is there a relationship that you're in at the moment that you need to get out of—fast?"*

iv. Keep it grace-filled

God is not into guilt. We need to be careful that our cutting application isn't just laying guilt upon our hearers. We need to phrase everything in the context of God's grace. We have a God who loves to forgive. We have a God who loves to see his children turn back to him. God is that heavenly Father waiting with open arms to hug you and welcome you and keep you by his side for ever.

3. The most important bit: "What is God really saying"?

Your great introduction—your witty illustrations—your thought-provoking application—none of these will make sense unless you get the message from God's word right! All of us can be guilty of twisting the Scriptures to make them say what we want them to say (I'm sure I've done that along the line!).

God urges us to be skilled in the way we handle his word:

> *Do your best to present yourself to God as one*
> *approved, a workman who does not need to be*
> *ashamed and who correctly handles the word of truth.*
> **2 Timothy 2:15**

How can you help to ensure that you get the message right? There are three vital steps. Don't miss any of them out!

a) What does the passage really say?

b) What does the passage really mean?

c) How does the passage really apply to this situation?

Let's look at those:

a) What does the passage really say?

This one requires a bit of work. But it really matters. You can't just jump to a passage and **guess** what you think it's saying! What it means **now** has to be consistent with what it meant **when it was first written**.

Follow these guidelines to help you get it right:

What did the original writer say to the original readers?

Read and re-read it **yourself**.

Hassle it through on your own.

Remember at this point, you're not trying to work out what the passage really **means**. You're simply trying to work out "What does it actually **say**?"

Here are some things that you'll need to take into account:

i. The background

Who wrote it?

To whom was it written?

Why was it written?

You can often find out these answers by reading the context—going back to the beginning of the book—or sometimes you might need to refer to a commentary so that you understand the original setting.

ii. The context

What comes immediately before and after the passage?

How does the passage fit into the book as a whole?

How does the passage fit into the Bible as a whole?

Never just grab a verse by itself and interpret it without reading the passages that come before and after it. Remember: *"A text without a context is a pretext"*.

iii. The style of literature

Different sorts of literature will present things in different ways. How you understand a historical section of the Bible (eg: Acts) will be different from how you understand a part of the Bible that is a song (eg: Psalms).

So what sort of literature is it? You might need to check with some commentaries to help you know how to understand it correctly.

Is it history, prose, poetry, proverb, allegory, parable, letter, prophecy, narrative, soliloquy, dialogue, apocalyptic… ?

iv. What do the words and phrases mean?

The original Bible was mainly written in Hebrew (Old Testament) and Greek (New Testament). What does the English word really mean? You don't need to be a language scholar to get this right! Simply check out your verse in a number of different English translations. This will help you to check that you're not misunderstanding a verse.

b) What does the passage really mean?

Now that you've worked out what the passage actually says to the original readers, you can take the second step, which is to determine "What did the passage really mean to the original readers?"

Check these out:

How are today's readers different or similar to the original hearers?

How is the world situation today different or similar to the society it was originally written to?

Look for the parallels!

c) How does the passage apply?

Much of this is covered in the previous section: "The took". The main reason for mentioning this step again is to emphasise—before you can work out how the Bible applies to **today's hearers**, you need to work through what it said and meant to the **original hearers**.

Check these out:

- *How is my situation different or similar to the original hearers?*

- *What does the passage say to me—where I am right at the moment?*

- *What does the passage say to my audience—where they are right at the moment?*

- *Don't forget the magic question—"So what?"*

Checkpoint: Are the conclusions that I draw from this passage similar to the conclusions the Bible itself draws?

4. Don't forget to finish!

Okay—you've done your hard work. You've worked through all the steps to ensure that you get the message right. You've got a great introduction, and you know how you're going to explore all the issues. You know how you're going to apply it to the lives of your hearers—so you're ready to go!

Well, not quite. There's another step or two to work through. This little bit of extra time you spend now can make your sermon or Bible study **so much better**.

Check it out!

a) Eliminate!

After you have gathered all your thoughts, written all your notes, collated all your cross-references, etc, etc, then you need to select what you will actually present to your audience. This will mean eliminating much good and useful material. This material may have been vital preparation, but it may not be necessary to spell it out in the actual study.

- *Can you simplify your points?*

- *Can you do an outline?*

- *Is there too much in it?*

- *Is it clear and concise?*

- *Does it make your main point clearly and simply?*

b) Plan your presentation
After you have worked out **what** to communicate, don't forget the second half of your preparation. You now need to determine **how** you are going to communicate it.

- *What methods will you use?*

- *How can you illustrate each point? (If you can't, then your audience certainly won't!)*

- *How will you begin?*

- *How will you finish?*

- *Are your methods suited to where the audience is at?*

- *Is the application clear?*

- *Is it too long or complicated?*

We are in the business of changing lives by the power of God's word. We have an awesome responsibility to be faithful and effective teachers of God's word.

When I first started preaching, I used to wonder: *"Why aren't busloads of people showing up to hear this?"* Now I look back at my early sermons, and I wonder: *"Why did anyone bother to show up and listen at all?"*

God is in charge! It is his word, and he brings the results. Sometimes we will find that God works **through** our Bible teaching, and sometimes we'll find that he works **despite** our Bible teaching!

But if you are a leader, then you are a Bible teacher. What an awesome privilege to be able to change this world—one life at a time!

For some helpful resources on how to understand and teach God's word, please refer to the recommendations in the Appendix 3 on page 303.

Chapter 15
You are a small-group leader

Youth leaders come in all shapes and sizes. There are all sorts of jobs to be done. There are all sorts of ministries that you need to be involved with. But **most likely** one of the first ways that you will become a Bible teacher is by leading a small group. You might lead a permanent Bible-study group—or it might be a looser arrangement where teenagers divide up into small groups for discussion at your youth group. It might even be that you are a leader in a camp, and your small group will be a "one off" arrangement that only lasts for the life of the camp.

Whatever it is, what are some ways of making your small group really effective? How can you be an impactful small-group leader?

1. Know your outline
You should have an outline—a rough sketch—of where you think you will go as you lead your small group.

Keep these checkpoints in mind:

a) What is your aim?

These important questions are often missed.

Why am I taking this Bible study?

What am I really hoping will be achieved?

When it is all over, what is the one result that I want people to walk away with?

b) What are your main points?
Refer back to Chapter 14, and identify your four main sections. Can you write a brief description of each? Can you list your key points under each section heading?

Do you remember the four main sections?

i. The hook ii. The book iii. The look iv. The took

c) How will you start… and finish?
Make sure you know where you are starting… and make sure you know where you want to end up.

2. Getting started

a) Sit together in as small a circle as is comfortable.

b) Make sure that you can see everyone's faces (so you can keep picking up feedback), and that everyone can see you (helps them to concentrate and to hear properly).

c) A group will always be more easily distracted outdoors—so stay indoors if you can. However, if you are taking a group outdoors:

> i. People sitting in the sun often become tired, lazy and frazzled. Despite the protests, a shaded area is usually better.

> ii. Make sure you face the sun, so your group will have their backs to it.

> iii. Don't have your group watching a distracting environment—eg: boats in the water, a chained-up dog etc.

d) How will you grab your group's attention with your **first** sentence?

e) If needed, agree on some ground rules so that your group will work.

3. Asking questions

One of the keys to being a successful small-group leader is to know how to ask questions. By asking questions wisely, you will help group members to discover important truths **for themselves**.

Try these tips for making your questions incisive:

a) Know what sort of question you are asking

There are lots of different sorts of questions. Both you and your members need to know what sort you are asking—so that you can end up with the answers you're after.

Here are eight different sorts of question which can help your group to achieve its aim. *(And just to make life interesting, all the examples given below are from an imaginary Bible study about "The Bible and alcohol!")*

i. Comprehension
What does the passage say?

This is especially used with younger teenagers who need "easy steps" to being involved in answering questions; eg:*"What does Jesus say about alcohol in verse 16?"* It can be a useful tool to help group members see what the text is actually **saying** before they start interpreting it. But be careful about over-using this style of question. If the answer is too obvious, group members will feel too embarrassed to answer! *"Look again in verse 20. Who dies on the cross for* *us?"* Hmmm. That might be the quickest way to kill your group!

ii. Interpretation
What does the passage mean?

This will help group members to think further. *"What do you think it really means when the Bible says to be 'filled with the Spirit?'"* The skilful use of interpretation questions can really help group members to come to grips with the passage for themselves.

iii. Application
How can you apply this to your life?

This is where you can help group members to start the "life change" that God's word demands. *"Think of some examples of how you can put this into action when you go to that party this weekend."* To be effective, application questions should always look for an answer which is both specific and personal.

iv. Rhetorical
No answer required!

Every now and again, a rhetorical question can add spice to your presentation. *"Does God want us to ruin our life?"* There is no answer needed. The answer is obvious. But be careful about over-doing it. Using too many rhetorical questions gets tiresome. And be careful about using rhetorical questions with very young students—they often feel the need to answer them! (This can really throw you!)

v. General knowledge
You get the answer from your general knowledge—not from the text.

When you're asking a general knowledge question, make it obvious that you want the answer to come from their own thinking, rather than from the text in front of them. *"So, what do you think God says about alcohol?"* is a general knowledge question.

vi. Value clarification
You help someone think through what they really believe.

"What's your attitude to under-age drinking?" "How do you feel when friends at a party start getting drunk" "What's more important to you—identifying with your friends by drinking too much with them, or identifying yourself as a Christian by keeping the law?"

vii. Clarifying question
To help someone be sure of their answer.

"So let me see if I understand what you're saying. You're saying alcohol is fine, but breaking the law and drunkenness aren't?"

viii. Summary question
See how much has been learned.

"Who can put into their own words what we think we've learned so far?"

b) Focus on feelings
Ask questions about group members' feelings on a subject, or about someone else's feelings. *"How do you feel when*

you get a really bad report card?" "How do you think Peter felt when the rooster crowed for the third time?"

As young people focus on feelings, they consider the subject in a personal way. They begin to understand how important the subject is to them, and that reinforces their attention.

c) Get students to question one another

Encourage your young people to challenge answers throughout the discussion session. *"What do you others think about that idea?" "Fred seems to be saying something a bit different from you—how do you respond to that?"*

As young people question each other, they move from the role of "students" to "seekers"—that is, they will learn to discover things for themselves. This can also help them to live with people regardless of disagreements.

d) Learn to interpret silence

Don't be afraid of silence. It's okay if everything goes quiet for a moment. Maybe your question wasn't understood. Try re-phrasing it or breaking it down into smaller questions. Maybe it means they are thinking. Give them this time.

e) Avoid "yes/no" questions

It will kill the discussion, force young people into one answer or another, and not require them to do any thinking. If you accidentally ask a question like this, try to follow immediately with a *"What sort of things make you feel that way?"* type question. (Which, by the way, is better than a "why" question.)

f) Keep encouraging
Keep highlighting the good answers that group members are giving. Give them good reinforcement, and this will make them feel more comfortable in discussing things—without worrying that they might be wrong.

g) Avoid judging
How do you deal with a wrong answer? Encourage the effort, and encourage what is right in their answer. Ask a clarifying question to push them further. *"I can understand why you might say that, but what do you think would happen if...?"* You can also get other group members to respond to a wrong answer.

4. General hints
a) If you want to ask a particular person a question, ask the question of the whole group, and then nominate the person to answer. Don't name the person before you ask the question, otherwise the rest of the group has no need to listen.

b) When asking questions to specific people, ask questions that you have confidence that they'll have the ability to answer.

c) Don't give all your attention to the noisy members. Involve the quiet ones as well.

d) Finish on time! (Write times next to your headings if necessary.)

e) Learn when to deal with distractions and when to ignore them.

f) Look at each person in the group.

g) Can you illustrate your major points? If you can't, then your group certainly won't be able to!

h) Work out all the probable wrong answers to questions you ask, the possible misinterpretations of the things you say, and any unfamiliar words or ideas. Simplify and clarify.

i) Be aware of the different Bible translations that people might be using. Make sure that the points you are making, and the answers you are expecting, are reasonably clear in other Bible versions.

j) Finally… if things aren't working out—for whatever reason—don't be scared to call for help. You are a member of a team, and there are plenty of others to assist you.

5. Handling difficult teenagers

In your small group there will be all sorts of members who will contribute helpfully to achieving your task. But there will some who are "less than helpful". Here are five difficult teenagers whom you'll meet in nearly every small group. How will you deal with them?

a) The dominator

This young person likes to be the boss, and their views and voice are always stronger than others. They answer every question—often correctly!

How do you deal with "the dominator"?

Acknowledge and support their contribution to the group.

Let them know that you appreciate the effort they're putting in.

Don't allow them to keep on answering everything: *"Let's hear from someone else."*

Invite others for their point of view.

Ask specific questions of specific people (especially if they've written their answers down first).

Quietly help them to see the need to be sensitive to others.

b) The silent one

This teenager just sits there. They rarely answer. They don't cause any trouble. But they don't get involved. And they don't help group life at all!

How do you deal with "the silent one"?

Try and work out why they're quiet. Are they bored? Are they shy? Spend some time with them outside the group, and get to know them better.

When they say something, encourage them. Silence is sometimes a sign of thinking things through deeply.

Get members to write answers down first. Then all "the silent one" has to do is "read their answer". This is much easier than making up an answer on the spot.

Allow them to be quiet in the group. Not everyone has to be talking all the time! But get them involved enough so that you know they're learning something.

c) The critic

This group member disagrees with everything and puts everyone down.

How do you deal with "the critic"?

Often this is a way of attracting attention. Do not allow your group to be a place where people are put down. Make this a guideline from the start.

Identify where it is **right** to be opposed to something, and support "the critic" in these instances.

Try to steer this young person to react against issues that need a strong negative response.

Don't allow them to dominate.

Understand their feelings, and allow the group to see that is one person's opinion: *"What's yours?"*

Give love and acceptance when they're not asking for it.

Catch up afterwards: *"What's worrying you? You seem a little unhappy with how things are done in our group."*

d) The disruptor
No matter what you do, this teenager always seems to disrupt your group and prevent you from achieving anything worthwhile.

How do you deal with "the disruptor"?

"Disruptors" will often seek attention by distracting the group. Try to give them attention before they ask for it.

Distinguish between behaviour which annoys you personally, and behaviour which disrupts the group.

Lay down guidelines at the beginning about the need for all of you to work together and co-operate. Remind the whole group of these rules.

Look for their good points and encourage them.

Catch up with them afterwards.

If they continue to disrupt the whole group, and show no sign of being helpful when you gently correct them, you may have to decide to temporarily exclude them from the group for the sake of the others. This can have a good effect on both the group and the individual (who can spend some personal time with a leader outside the group).

e) The clown

This young person makes jokes about everything, all the time.

How do you deal with "the clown"?

Encourage their sense of humour, and join in with it where you can.

Encourage the whole group toward maturity—knowing when it's great to have a laugh, and knowing when it's time to stop.

Give them attention when they don't ask for it.

Ask: *"What would happen if you took this seriously instead of making a joke about it?"* Humour is often a way of avoiding the real issues.

Talk with them outside the group.

Leading a small group is a huge privilege. You get to disciple the Christian leaders of the next generation. You enter into a unique and personal relationship with each student—at a time when they're often not that receptive to other adults in their life. You get to mould and shape a young believer, and set them on a course of maturity and faithfulness which will last their whole life.

This position is an awesome privilege. I know you will take it seriously and teach the Bible well in your small group so that lives are changed for eternity.

For leaders who are serious about developing disciples in small groups, I refer you to "The role of the coach" on page 234 in "Fruit That Will Last".

Chapter 16

You are building a leadership team

I want you to imagine a *Rambo* movie. Doesn't matter which one. They're all pretty much the same. In the middle of a fierce battle, our boys have been taken captive by the evil enemy dictator. They are being held at some savage, brutal POW camp deep in an unknown jungle. After several efforts, the top brass have given up on ever finding these men. They cannot even locate the POW camp. They call off the rescue mission and simply list our soldiers as "missing in action".

But this is not good enough for John Rambo! He takes off **by himself**. He single-handedly locates that enemy POW camp. All by himself he breaks into that camp and rescues every one of "our boys". He overcomes every guard with sheer determination and a large knife clenched between his teeth. He completes his victory by tossing his last hand grenade into the ammo dump; then he escapes with every POW in tow, against the backdrop of the entire camp being blown sky-high as it explodes in a gi-normous fireball. The film finishes with a huge ticker-tape reception—with a giant flag fluttering in the background, with personal congratulations from the president himself.

Lots of youth ministries operate like that. They have a dynamic youth pastor who will not accept the complacency of the fuddy-duddies at their church. Our intrepid youth pastor goes out on **single-handed raids** and rescues kids from Satan's prison. All by himself he restocks his church with the generation of today. He receives accolades for his daring work into unchartered territory.

When I first started in youth ministry, I guess I thought of myself that way. What glory there would be when I went where no youth pastor had dared to go, and approached the unapproachable, redeemed the unredeemable, restored the unrestorable, and achieved the unachievable.

You know the problem with Rambo-style youth ministries? When the dynamic whizz-kid that's running it leaves—or is sacked—the whole thing collapses.

Jesus didn't do that. He didn't spend his three-year ministry racing around winning the whole world single-handedly. He didn't set up ministry programmes that attracted the crowds and dazzled them with his style. His aim was not to have a spectacular three-year ministry and then see the whole thing collapse when he left. His aim was to make disciples of all nations so that, because of these three years of ministry, every person in every land—and in every era—would hear about his saving work on the cross and be challenged to respond.

Jesus wasn't just here to single-handedly have a spectacular mission. He was here to train a leadership team. His motley collection of doctors, fishermen, tax-collectors and political wannabe's was transformed by him so that they could transform this world throughout every generation.

It's no use just being a leader. You need to be effective enough raise up **a whole army of other leaders** who will operate in conjunction with you. You need to create a culture where leadership bubbles to the surface, and is encouraged and spurred on by you so that the ministry of those around you can even overtake what you yourself can achieve.

You're not a leader because you can attract followers to join up with you. You're a leader when you can attract and raise up other **leaders** to join up with you.

You don't just want a bunch of students who are attracted to what you do. You don't really want a collection of helpers who will assist you in your ministry. You don't even want a team of leaders who can "keep the ship afloat" for a few years after you've gone.

You want to raise up a generation of leaders who will run the ministry better and richer and deeper and with more impact than you ever could.

My firm belief is that if I suddenly met an untimely demise—and I was no longer available to help resource our local church youth ministry—after a brief time of intense sadness, our youth ministry would carry on without a hiccough!

How do you raise up a leadership team around you? How do you create a culture which encourages leadership to rise to the top? How do you achieve the most important aspect of leadership—to ensure that it grows and prospers long after you are just a dim, distant memory?

1. Build with care

But we were gentle among you, like a mother caring
for her little children.   *1 Thessalonians 2:7*

Ministry is always about people. Always. And people need to be cared for. The key group of people to care for are your **leaders**. Do you want to build a leadership team? Then start by caring for them.

a) People are more valuable than the ministry they produce

Your people really matter. Your people really need to be cared for. Your people need to have time spent with them.

The same is true of your leaders!

Your leaders are valuable as people. They're not just valuable because of the ministry they can produce.

It can be a real temptation in ministry to value people because of the ministry they produce for you. You look after them because no one can run games like they can. You keep people onside because you don't want to end up running the youth group by yourself.

That is not genuine care. It really matters to value your people **simply because of who they are**, not because they help you achieve your aims. When people know and feel that they are valued—simply for being themselves—then they are motivated to be strong leaders and have an awesome ministry.

I'm not good at this. My "mercy" gifts are way down the list. My immediate team probably suffers because this is not one of my natural strengths. But if you find that genuine caring is not one of your natural strengths, then there is a need to be even more disciplined so that you do take the time to care for them individually.

b) Caring for your leaders is more important than caring for your group members

When I first started out in youth-ministry world, I never believed this. **I was there for the teenagers!** Other leaders would help me. I imagined that the role of other leaders was to help me spend more quality time with students! It **has** to be the other way around. If I only want to care for teenagers, then the number of young people I can impact for Christ will always be limited to the number I can personally care for. This is one of the key reasons why so many church youth groups across the world never grow to more than a few dozen teenagers. But when you shift your focus so that your prime emphasis is to care for and develop your **leaders**, then there is no limit to the number of young people who can be cared for as your leadership team grows.

Caring for your leaders is more important than caring for your group members. How do I know this? **Because that's what Jesus did!** Yes, he was constantly there for all sorts of people who needed him—but his primary focus for his three years of public ministry was to build his leadership team.

c) Don't try to care for everyone

You need to have a structure to make sure that you're not having to care for too many people. Because if you're trying to care for too many, then none of them will be cared for well. And then they in turn will not be empowered to care well for those who work with them.

It's easy when your youth group is just you and five kids. You simply care for the five kids. What about when you've got thirty kids and five leaders? Easy! You care for the five leaders. Each leader cares for six kids. But what about when you have 100 leaders? And 300, 400, or 500 kids? How do you make sure that everyone gets cared for?

As a full-time youth pastor at a local church with a large youth ministry, I had four youth staff. They were my primary group. They were the ones I attempted to care for. Each one of them had around four volunteer team-leaders that they would care for. Each one of those team-leaders had up to half a dozen front-line leaders whom they would care for. Each one of those leaders had 6-10 teenagers they would care for. That's how we made sure that **everyone got cared for**.

If you have a whole stack of people who are answerable to you, can you restructure things so you can care deeply for no more than six?

Back at your church… are there some leaders whom you need to spend some individual time with? Are there some leaders where you've valued their output more than who they are as a person? Are there some leaders whom you simply need to care for?

2. Build with words

The tongue has the power of life and death.

Proverbs 18:21

Words are so powerful. They can build people up or push people down. The words that you speak can be such an encouragement to your leaders. Do you want to build a leadership team? Then sow words of life into them.

a) Sow words of life

Everything you say can either build people up or push people down. Everything you say can either draw your leaders closer or push them further away.

I have to admit—sometimes I don't always do too well here. I have a sense of humour which can be quite sarcastic and caustic. I grew up in a family where we would slice each other to pieces with our words. It was real one-upmanship to be able to pay out better than what you'd just been dumped with. And it can be very funny. But it always hurts. Everything you say will either draw others closer to you, or push them further away. Here's the problem with sarcastic humour—it always pushes people away.

I want to make sure that the words I speak to others—especially to my leaders—are **words of life**. Will you join with me in this—and build up your leaders the same way?

b) Sow words of encouragement

We were running our week-long camp. I had asked one of my trusted leaders to reinvigorate our worship music. I felt we needed to really lift our standard so we could help our young people have their hearts set on fire for Jesus. As the camp progressed, I noticed how well we were doing with that. I was so proud of Craig, the leader whom I had asked to oversee and develop our "Rage 'n' Praise" band.

On around day three, Craig my music leader, was chatting with me. He said: *"I get the feeling that you're not very happy with what I'm doing with our music"*. I instantly replied: *"What on earth gave you the idea that I wasn't happy with it?"* His answer? *"You haven't said anything about it to me all week!"*

How could I do that? I was delighted with his efforts and result **but I had not told him**! Aarrgghh!! Sometimes encouragement is as simple as saying to a person what you are thinking already.

We have a number of youth leaders who are in their very early stages of preaching at our youth group. Usually when they are preaching, I am taking notes to help me with my feedback to them. But after a while I worked out that while they were preaching, when they glanced at me in the crowd for just a moment, if all they ever saw was my head buried in my notebook as I scribbled things down, then at the very moment of preaching they would get no positive affirmation back from me. What I try to do now is that as well as taking notes, I make eye-contact with them while they are preaching, so that when their glance catches mine, they will see me nodding and smiling—and giving them instant encouragement as they continue on out the front.

Words of encouragement are **so vital**! If you want to build a champion leadership team, learn to be a champion encourager.

c) Give private and public recognition

Private encouragement is fantastic, but you move it to a whole new level when you encourage your leaders **publicly**! On our Crossfire leadership team, we usually have a leaders' meeting before and after our Friday-night youth group. What we will sometimes do is publicly encourage our leaders. If our Year 9 leaders have run a lot of the programme that night, we might sit our Year 9 leaders in the middle of the whole leadership team, and go around and publicly affirm the good things that they did that night. Then we can pray for each of them individually as we support them in their leadership role.

d) The most important words of leadership

The five most important words of leadership:
"You did a great job".

The four most important words of leadership:
"What do you think?"

The three most important words of leadership:
"Could you please…?"

The two most important words of leadership: *"Thank you"*.

The one most important word of leadership: *"We"*.

Did you notice the least important word of leadership? *"I"*.

Back at your church: Which leaders do you need to go to and give a word of private encouragement? Which leaders do you need to applaud publicly? If you want to build a dynamic leadership team—then continue to sow words of life into them!

3. Build with training

Some years ago, as our youth group was finishing, a Year 7 boy came up to me and said: *"Tim, I think I want to become a Christian"*. Well—you didn't have to give me any more encouragement than this. I sat down with him. I asked him questions. I helped him clarify his decision. He seemed absolutely ready to make this move. I prayed with him; he gave his heart to Jesus; his eternity was changed! I sent him away with assurance of follow-up and ongoing discipleship. Yee-hah!

The next morning I thought to myself: *"What have I done?"* There was nothing wrong with the procedure I had taken, but here's the problem: **I had done it by myself**! There was nobody else there assisting and helping. There was no one else watching and learning how to do this ministry. And while the Year 7 boy had been led in all the right directions, **I had wasted a ministry-training opportunity** by not getting someone else involved. At that moment I made a commitment: never again would I do a ministry like that solo. I would **always** seek to involve someone else so that I didn't miss a ministry training opportunity.

A few months later, at our annual camp, a Year 8 boy came up to me and said: *"I think I want to become a Christian".* *"Fantastic!"* I replied. *"Who here is one of your good friends?"* He pointed out his Year 8 friend James, who was standing nearby. James was a young Christian who was a member of my Year 8 Boys' Discipleship Team.

"Hey James—I need your help! Doug wants to talk about becoming a Christian. Can you help me?"

So James—all of 13 years old—sat down with us. He listened; he prayed; he encouraged. And as his friend gave his life to Christ, James learned how to do ministry.

When I say "Build With Training", your thoughts may well go to gathering your leaders for a classroom training lesson. And there is nothing wrong with that! But here I am talking about another sort of training. If you genuinely want to grow a leadership team, can you **build in hands-on training at every ministry opportunity**? That is, every time you, or someone on your team, exercises a ministry, can they have someone else with them watching and learning?

Any ministry which is a solo ministry is a wasted ministry.

Look at the ministry of Jesus. Let's take a quick trip through two chapters of Luke's Gospel—and notice how he builds in training at every ministry opportunity.

Luke 8

> v 1: *As Jesus travels from village to village,* **the twelve are with him**. *Why?*

v 9: *After Jesus teaches the parable of the sower, he explains it privately to the twelve.*

v 22: *Before Jesus calms the storm, the disciples need to wake him. Why?*

v 45: *When Jesus heals the woman who is bleeding, it is Peter who jumps in with an explanation.*

v 51: *When Jesus is about to raise Jairus' daughter, he takes Peter, James and John in with him. Why?*

Luke 9

v 1: *Jesus sends the twelve out to do ministry without him. (Does this answer some of the "why" questions?)*

v 12: *Feeding the 5000. Jesus waits for the disciples to bring the problem to him. Then he invites the disciples to be part of the problem-solving team. Then, when he distributes the food, he involves the disciples in the miraculous process. They are the ones who give the food out to the crowd.*

v 18: *Jesus is described as "praying in private"—**but his disciples were with him**. Why?*

v 20: *Jesus directly asks his disciples what they think about him.*

v 22: *Jesus teaches his disciples about the cost of discipleship.*

v 28: *Jesus takes Peter, James and John with him to see him transfigured. Why?*

v 38: *The disciples try out some ministry—and Jesus gets called in when they get it wrong.*

v 46: *Jesus teaches his disciples about genuine leadership.*

v 49: *Jesus allows John to ask questions about ministry—and then corrects him.*

v 54: *Jesus allows James and John to make suggestions about ministry strategy—and then corrects them.*

Luke 10

v 1: *Jesus sends the 72 to go and minister in pairs— without him. (Does this answer some of the "why" questions?)*

Are you picking up the pattern? Can you see how Jesus is building leadership training into every ministry he does. There is always someone watching him, asking him, and then trying it themselves.

Can you see the progression?

8:1: *Jesus is doing the ministry—with the twelve in tow.*

9:1: *Jesus sends the twelve out to minister without him.*

10:1: *Jesus send out the seventy two to minister without him.*

I have often wondered where the 72 came from. Scripture does not tell us. But just suppose for a moment that each disciple went and trained six others, just as Jesus had trained them. That would make 72. The Scriptures do not give the details of this, but it is obvious from Jesus' ministry that **as he does ministry, he also trains his twelve how to do it as well**. That's how we can go from Jesus by himself at the beginning of Luke 8… to the twelve ministering at the beginning of Luke 9… to the seventy two ministering at the beginning of Luke 10. On-the-job training is built in at every opportunity.

Back at your church: Are there some ministries that you are doing solo which you can involve your team in? Can you build in training with every ministry that happens? If you really want to develop a great leadership team, then build them with training.

4. Build with expectation

If you're going to build a leadership team for the future, then you need to keep raising their expectations for what the future holds. A leadership team that is only committed to the mediocre is a leadership team going nowhere!

a) Set the bar high

If you want to build a leadership team, you need to set a high but realistic expectation of your leaders. Are they committed for the whole year? If there's a meeting—are they there? Are they on time? Have they prepared what they said they'd prepare? You want to model love, grace and forgiveness. But set the expectation high. And encourage like crazy to keep it there. You will never build a leadership team if you set the bar at mediocrity. You are better having a smaller number of leaders with a higher commitment, than a larger number of leaders with a half-hearted commitment.

When I started at my church as youth pastor, I found a high resistance level amongst my existing youth leaders. What did I mean: *"Let's have some training"*? It seemed to be part of the culture to show up late, come when you feel like it, prepare at the last minute, and generally put in the bare minimum. Despite my best efforts, and my deepest enthusiasm, my leaders seemed resistant to any attempt to raise the bar.

So eventually, I had to resort to Plan B. I worked on those **who were not yet leaders**. I started to sow new aspirations for leadership in our high-schoolers. I started a leadership training course to prepare them for the day when they would join our adult leadership team. I started with all the people who **wanted** to be leaders, but had not yet made the step. Any new or potential leader was challenged with high standards, and shown what their commitment really meant. They understood the value of training and reliability.

In the first year that these newly-trained leaders came on board, they represented about 5% of my entire leadership team. In Year 2 they represented about 10%. By the time we got to Year 5, they represented around 90% of the entire leadership team. Over a five-year period we had turned the complete leadership culture around.

b) It's okay to fail

If you're going to build a culture where you set the bar high, then you have to also set a culture where it's okay to try something—and fail. If it's not okay to fail, your leaders will always plan for safety—and will drift back to mediocrity. You can set this standard that it's okay to try something, and then admit it might not have been the best idea, by being honest with your **own** ideas that you bring to the youth ministry. There have been many times where I have gone to my team and said: *"You know that new idea that we started this year? I don't think I steered us on the right course. Can we have another look at it?"*

If it's not okay to fail, no one will try anything. After all, Jesus let his disciples fail at ministry!

c) The best is yet to come
If you want to inspire your leadership team, you must always believe that the place God is leading you to is better than the place he is leading you from. That is always the way our God works. He is a God of the future. He always takes us forward. So, look to the future. Always build with the possibilities in mind. Don't rest on past glories.

"Remember the good old days of our youth group? It'll never be like that again!"

"Times have changed. We used to get 300 kids to Sunday School in the 1950's. We'll never do that again!"

Why not?

Maybe it won't be a Sunday School, but why can't God lead you to have a ministry to 300 kids… or 500 kids… or…?

If you think God has finished with you and your youth ministry—close it down! But always build with big expectations in mind.

d) The best is yet to come—for your emerging leaders
If you're growing leaders under your wing, then you are always looking at where God is taking them to, rather than where God is taking them from. Your leaders will always make mistakes. They will often leave things to the last moment. They will sometimes run things at a lower standard than what you would. Sometimes they will be impatient; jump the gun; get carried away with their own success; or fire their mouth off before they put their brain into action.

You can deal with that. If Jesus could deal with Peter, then you can deal with your less-than-perfect leaders. I'm sure Jesus had his eyes on the leader that Peter would become, rather than always reminding him of the failures he had made in the past.

Back at your church: Are there some leaders who you need to start seeing with the eye of faith—as to who they are becoming, rather than who they once were? Are there some expectations you need to raise amongst your leadership team so that you lift the bar for your whole youth ministry? Do you need to move your team out of "the good old days"—and focus them on "the best is yet to come"?

5. Build with prayer

Paul makes a remarkable statement when he writes to the Christians at Colossae:

> *For this reason, since the day we heard about you, we have not stopped praying for you.* **Colossians 1:9**

Can you say that about the leaders on your team? That from the day you first heard about them, you have not stopped praying for them? Yes—you need to pray for your young people. But first of all, start praying for your leaders!

And look at what Paul prays for!

> *For this reason, since the day we heard about you, we have not stopped praying for you and asking God to fill you with the knowledge of his will through all spiritual wisdom and understanding. And we pray this in order that you may live a life worthy of the Lord and may please him in every way: bearing fruit in every good work, growing in the knowledge of God, being strengthened with all power according to his*

*glorious might so that you may have great endurance
and patience, and joyfully giving thanks to the Father,
who has qualified you to share in the inheritance of
the saints in the kingdom of light.* **Colossians 1:9-12**

Does this match up with the sorts of things that you pray
for your leaders? Or do you need to adjust something in
your prayers to bring them more into line with the biblical
model?

How do you build a leadership culture? How do you help
create an environment where leadership bubbles to the top
in the people around you? How do you inspire many others
to join you in leadership so that together you accomplish far
more than you ever could by yourself?

Build with care.

Build with words.

Build with training.

Build with expectation.

Build with prayer.

God is not just calling on you to be a leader. He is calling on
you to raise a whole army of leaders who will minister for
him on this planet! You are not just building a ministry. You
are building a whole leadership team!

Chapter 17

You are many, many people

When you step into ministry as a Christian youth leader, you step into a strange world. While you will always be your own person, living in a genuine way and not just changing to suit the circumstances, you will be called upon to take many different roles.

We have explored many of these leadership roles already. You are a shepherd... you are a servant... you are a Bible teacher...

Here is a collection of just some of the roles you might be called upon to take in this strange world called "youth leadership".

1. You are a pray-er

When we look in the Bible, we see how vital the ministry of prayer is. Listen to Paul as he talks about the role of prayer in his ministry:

> *For this reason, since the day we heard about you, we have not stopped praying for you and asking God to fill you with the knowledge of his will through all spiritual wisdom and understanding.* **Colossians 1:9**

> *Brothers, my heart's desire and prayer to God for the Israelites is that they may be saved.* **Romans 10:1**

If you really want to see the sort of prayer that Paul prayed for those whom he ministered to, then check out Ephesians 3:14-21.

Prayer is so vital if you're going to be a youth leader. Pray for your own walk with Jesus.

Pray for your ministry. Pray for your team. Pray for your young people.

If you want to see God in action—ask him! A Christian leader should be a champion pray-er. If you do nothing more than pray faithfully and regularly for your group members, then you will see mighty things happen in their lives as God answers your prayers.

2. You are a growing disciple

A Christian leader is like a water-tank. There is a tap at the bottom, and the water supply—from rain etc—comes in at the top. Every time that tap is turned on, some of the water in the tank drains out. If it is not being refilled from the top, then it will last for a while, but eventually it will run dry.

If you are constantly being "drained" as a Christian leader, then you need to make sure you are being "filled up" as well. If you're always giving out, and yet never taking in, then you might last for a while, but eventually you will run dry.

It really matters that you look after your own Christian life and make sure that you keep growing. You need to be faithful in your own personal worship; you need to be faithful in your own Bible-study group; and you need to be faithful at church.

If you give up growing as God's child, then you won't be able to help anyone else grow. Because they will always turn out like you. And if you've stopped growing, then guess what? The students you disciple will stop growing as well!

3. You are a learner

In one sense, none of us has ever made it. You are always a learner as a disciple. You are always a learner as a leader. No matter how long you have been a leader—and how much you have learned about being a leader—there is always more that God wants to teach you.

I've been a full-time youth pastor in a local church for over thirty years. I go to every conference on youth ministry that I can—and I take my team with me. Often I will be listening to a lecture taken by a young youth pastor who has been in the ministry for three years, teaching me about youth leadership. I could go with the attitude of *"What can this young punk possibly teach me?"*, but I'd much rather go with the attitude *"What does God want to teach me today?"* And you know, whenever I go with that attitude, **God always teaches me something**!

"Leaders are readers"—that's how the saying goes. I guess it's true (after all—it rhymes!) But can I let you in on a little secret? I don't read that much! *(Gulp! The secret's out now!)* One of my staff members once commented to me: *"Tim—I think you've written more books than you've read"*. You know, it's pretty close to the truth! For some reason, I just don't learn well from reading. I certainly don't **enjoy** reading. (In fact, if I hadn't written **this** book, I would probably never read it! So congratulations on getting this far! You are awesome!)

But I certainly learn from going to conferences! I certainly learn from sitting down with other youth pastors and picking their brains about what they are doing in ministry at the moment. I certainly learn by listening to what God is doing in other people's lives.

"Leaders are readers"? Perhaps. I prefer this one: *"Leaders are learners"*. (It doesn't rhyme, but it alliterates!) Find the way that you learn the best—and pursue it as far as you can. Keep learning about leadership. God still has much to teach you.

A leader who stops learning should stop leading!

4. You are a planner

There are two things that work against youth leaders being good planners:

Today's young generation likes to be spontaneous.

Today's Christian generation likes to be "led by the Spirit"— just "go where he leads".

I love spontaneity. I love being led by God's Spirit. But the thing that enables me to be spontaneous—and the thing that enables me to be Spirit-led—is that I am well-planned! Because when you plan well—**the important things get to happen!**

Sometimes you can get away without doing much planning. If you are in a solo ministry—and no one much else is depending on you—you can be very spur of the moment, and no one will worry too much. **But as soon as you are in a team ministry—with others depending on you—then you let everyone down when you don't plan effectively.**

What tasks have you got in youth ministry? **Plan them with excellence!** Are you responsible for planning a game or an activity for your youth group? **Plan it well!** Do you need to lead a Bible-study group? **Plan it well!** Do you need to catch up with individual students to follow them up? **Plan it well!**

Planning well means that you plan **well ahead**—and don't leave things to the last moment. When you leave things to the last moment, you make life difficult for every one of your fellow leaders.

Planning well means that you **plan thoroughly**. Have you organised an outdoor activity? Then you should have planned a wet-weather alternative. Are you planning an outing somewhere? Then you should have planned the transport arrangements. Are you planning a camp? Then you should have planned for safety precautions and first aid.

Planning well means you **plan with excellence**. Imagine you are responsible for planning the opening activity at your Friday-night youth group. What happens if you don't plan it well? The whole night is dragged down—and every other ministry is dragged down with you.

If you fail to plan, then you plan to fail!

5. You are a meeting-attender

Every ministry needs to have meetings so that the team can come together—plan together, pray together and move forward together.

Maybe you love meetings—maybe you don't. But if you're involved in leadership, it really matters that you honour the meetings that are called for that ministry.

Turn up to your meeting on time. The meeting is an important time of communication and preparation. It is the beginning of a successful night, and a lack of attendance may mean a lack of success. Come prepared for anything you are to do that night. Join with your team in prayer for it is only through God that we can achieve anything in ministry!

6. You are an organiser

Be aware of things that need to be set up. Help your team organise welcoming group members... or collecting money... or running activities... whatever! There will always be heaps to do!

Be prepared if you are the next person on the running sheet. Get up near the front ready to take over. Don't let the person up front look lost. Be there and be ready!

Whatever needs to happen to make your youth ministry run smoothly, be ready to lend a hand—even if it's not your responsibility. We all need to pull together—and as servants together, we can achieve great things in ministry.

7. You are a crowd-controller

When your youth ministry programme starts, get in there among the young people ready to relate to them. Make sure you are always surrounded by students—**not leaders**! Help to keep the group quiet when it is time for them to listen. Support the person up front by modelling the behaviour you want the young people to display. Don't leave everything to the person up the front. Teenagers are usually lively, restless, full of life and energy. So don't be scared to take the initiative to help things go smoothly.

8. You are a participator

Activities and games will not work if leaders are not involved. If leaders say they don't want to participate, then be assured that the young people will say the same!

So whatever your youth group is doing—**join in**! Maybe it's your favourite activity—maybe it isn't. **But it needs you enthusiastically involved—and it needs you to be positive!** Never speak negatively about an activity or game as your negativity will rub off onto your group. And who wants to be part of a negative youth group?

I have a personal confession to make here. I don't particularly like cricket. I can't bowl well; I can't bat well; I can't field well. (This sort of limits my cricket opportunities!) I like games that start with a whistle and finish about an hour and a half later. To me, cricket just seems like baseball played under valium!

I was a cabin leader on a Year 7 camp. I was looking after a bunch of 12-year-old boys who were full of life and energy. And guess what?

They were mad keen on cricket!

So as a cricket-hating leader—what did I do? We organised ourselves into a cricket team. There had been bushfires around the campsite, and there was plenty of black charcoaled wood to be found. We went out and rubbed this on our faces until they were black—we called ourselves "The Worst Indies"—and we challenged every other cabin to a cricket competition. I never let on about my personal dislike of cricket. I jumped in feet first and led my boys.

You are a participator. So join in!

9. You are a group leader

At some stage you will be responsible for a section of your youth ministry. Maybe a small group. Maybe an age-based group. Maybe a geographically-based group. But whatever it is, work hard to build the community in that group. Build the relationships in your group.

Look for ways to build group identity in your group. Encourage healthy competition with the other groups—in things such as games, attendance, newcomers etc. Your particular group is the community where young people will feel they belong. Make it a place where they feel welcomed, and where they will want to bring friends.

10. You are a disciplinarian

This can be a ministry that is difficult for many of us but it is necessary for a successful night. You can be a teenager's friend as well as being a firm leader.

Don't leave all the discipline to another leader. All the team should work together on this.

If a young person is misbehaving…

- tell them it is not appropriate—tell them that you need them to stop.

- sit near them to help prevent the behaviour.

- sit just behind them when everyone is facing the front.

- give them a second warning.

If they are not responding, take them to your immediate supervisor. Then that young person can have individual attention, and you can continue ministering to the rest of the group.

Teenagers need to be pulled back when they are being disrespectful, rude or a nuisance. The team needs to work together to ensure bad behaviour does not become a major problem. It will help to have your discipline procedure written down so that every member of the team knows what it is—and sticks to it! You will also need to ensure that you work within the child-protection policy of your church or organisation.

11. You are a hang-er
One of the most effective ministries is one to one and happens usually in the unstructured time in your youth group. This "hang time" is where friendships are built.

Use it wisely!

Always be with the young people. If you are always with other leaders, there is something wrong. Leaders talking to leaders usually means **no ministry is happening**.

Don't be afraid to hang around. While not every student will want to stay and talk, there will be many who appreciate an adult taking an interest in them.

12. You are a friend
Develop genuine relationships with your young people. Show an interest in them, and in what they're doing. Have contact with them outside your youth group time.

Just be there for them. Be there as they stand and chat. Be there in "hang time". Be there at their Grand Final. Be there when their parents are splitting up. Be there when they're facing their big exams. Be there as they discover Jesus.

13. You are a listener
You don't need a fancy degree in psychology. You don't need to be a trained counsellor. Both these people are important—and you may well need them to be around—

but most of the time, all your group members need for you to do is to **listen** to them.

They don't need you to solve all their problems; they don't always need your advice; they don't need you to make decisions for them; they don't need you to run their life; they don't expect that you will know exactly how they feel (you never will!)—but they do need you to let them know that you understand that they might be going through a difficult time.

Simply take the time to listen. Notice I did not say: *"Take the time to talk to them"*. Take the time to listen. Two ears, one mouth—you get the ratio?

14. You are a role model

You will not be perfect. You will make mistakes. But that's exactly the sort of role model a young person needs! They need to have someone they look up to **who makes mistakes just like they do**. How you **deal** with your mistakes really matters. Your students need to see you model repentance, forgiveness and restoration. They will watch you when you are doing well—and they will watch you when you aren't doing so well.

They say that young people don't like listening to their elders. But I can assure you they always **imitate** their elders. Scary thought, eh? So make sure you are living a life that is **worth copying**!

15. You are a witness

A Christian doesn't "do" witnessing. A Christian **is** a witness. You might be a good witness or an ineffective witness—but you are always a witness for Jesus. 24/7.

You might be the only contact your group members have with a Christian on a regular basis. Think about that! **The only version of the Bible that some of them might ever read is you!** What a privilege! What a responsibility!

So as you develop great relationships with your group, make sure that you introduce them to the greatest relationship they could ever have—a saving relationship with their Lord and God, Jesus Christ.

You are a witness. **Wow**!

16. You are a team member

God rarely calls us to minister solo; God is very much into teams. He is a team within himself—Father, Son and Holy Spirit. He places his people into a body of believers. Nearly every ministry you do will be in the context of teamwork with other Christians.

Pray for your team. Support your team leaders and their decisions. Don't let your team down. Encourage and love each other as Christian brothers and sisters. Work as a team to maintain excellence, discipline and ministry for God's glory.

Chapter 18

You are a leader who will last

Surviving the five stages of youth ministry

Imagine this situation: Fred is the new youth pastor at St. Blogg's Church of the Holy Revival. With a few years of Bible college behind him, he launches himself into the tumultuous world of young people and starts running some stunningly successful-looking youth programmes. The worship band is hot; the talks are powerful; the relationships are deep; the donuts are "awesome".

But there is some friction. Old Mrs Battersby doesn't like what "those young people" are doing to "her" church service. Senior Pastor Gizmo has high expectations of his new youth pastor, but unfortunately the numbers level off after the initial six-month burst. The children's ministry is jealous because young Fred is taking all "their" leaders. Many Christian parents are worried about all those "new" kids who have been attracted to "their" youth programmes. And the hard-working Fred finds that his group often let him down, and can't be relied upon to do their bit to make the whole thing work.

Poor old youth pastor Fred is starting to ask questions as to whether he is really in the place that God has called him to. Things aren't quite working out the way he had hoped.

But there is a solution at hand! There is a church on the other side of town that calls Fred and asks him to be **their** youth pastor. This could be the answer to his prayers! All the signs are there that this is a genuine call from God! It's a nicer area, with a bigger youth group and a more generous salary!

So even though he has only been at St. Blogg's for 18 months, youth pastor Fred pulls out, and heads off to a better-looking church where he might find his ecclesiastical fame and fortune. Except the same things happen. The same discouragements. The same feeling of being isolated and unappreciated. And Fred is feeling a bit older now—maybe too old for youth ministry. So despite his Bible-college training—despite his initial enthusiasm—after three years he is no longer in youth ministry, and to be quite honest, not nearly as keen a Christian as he used to be.

An outrageous story? No. **This is the typical life-cycle of so many youth pastors in the world.** Often in youth ministry for no longer than three years. Often never in the same church for more than eighteen months. Discouraged. Withdrawn. Burnt out. Given up.

And for the volunteer youth leader, the figures are worse. Often they stay no longer than a year as a youth leader, before pulling out and going on to other things which require less strain and emotional energy.

Try this sometime. Go to a conference on youth ministry, and try to find youth pastors who have been at the same church for more than three years. There aren't that many. I know. I go to a lot of youth-ministry conferences!

When you look at all this, you have to admit that something's going wrong. If the medical profession was evolving like this—where no doctor stayed as a physician for longer than three years—then we'd be in a bad way. Would we have any doctors? Of course! Would we have any **good** doctors? No way!

I feel distressed when I see youth pastors and youth leaders dropping out of youth ministry **long before they ever get good at it**! We have an emerging generation of young people who desperately need to know the love of Jesus, and have their destinies changed for eternity. We have a culture that is increasingly feeling alienated from traditional church values. We need an army of workers who are committed **long term** to seeing this new generation take their place as leaders in God's community.

Here is my challenge to everyone who is involved in youth ministry: ***"Will you stay in youth ministry long enough to get it right?"*** Will you hang in there as you grow in wisdom and maturity so that you will be able to teach and model to the upcoming generation what it means to be committed long term to the youth of this world? Will you go along with the flow of "incredibly short-term youth ministries", or will you **break** this mould and start a whole new culture of being committed to young people **long term**?

I am absolutely convinced that the most effective youth ministry is long-term youth ministry. The longer you stay in it—the better it gets. The longer you stay in it—the better **you** get. The longer you stay in it—the **easier** it gets! (Does that sound appealing?)

So, if all this is true, then why don't more youth pastors and youth leaders stay in this vital ministry longer?

I think there are two main reasons:

They don't really understand the biblical ministry that God has called them to. *(And please, if you haven't read it already, can I recommend you have a thorough read of "Fruit That Will Last"?!)*

They don't understand how the way you do youth ministry changes as you get older. *(Read on!)*

As you get older, your role will change. I want you to be aware of these changes. If you don't make these changes, you will not last long. There are five distinct phases that you will go through if you've committed to ministering to youth long-term.

God can use people at **every one** of these five stages. There are no good stages or bad stages—they are merely different from each other. You need to be aware of the advantages—and the limitations—of each stage. I believe we need youth leaders **in all five of these stages**. What I sadly notice at many churches is that you rarely get leaders in anything except Stages 1 and 2.

Stage 1: The "one of the gang" stage

This is where you are a young youth leader of (say) 18, and the students you lead are about 16. There are only a few years' difference between you and them. You know their culture well because you live in their culture. You like the same music as the kids; you wear the same clothes; you do the same things. You laugh at the same jokes; you commit the same sins; you get bored by the same sermons. You are always at each other's parties, and the group members have no problem at all in including you as one of their best friends.

a) Advantages of this stage

You will often have instant acceptance by students and you will have easy accessibility to everything they do. You will identify with the group strongly, and passionately argue their causes for them. They will see you as being incredibly "cool". You will be quickly admired—you are "just like them"—except you have a little more money, you have a car, you have the privileges and freedoms of adulthood, and you have fewer facial skin imperfections!

You will probably have oodles of energy and be able to join in (and outlast!) practically everything your group members do. You will still have an idealism where you know that the world **can** be changed—and you won't let tradition get in your way of doing things better. You may well be full of life—and optimism—and will inspire your group to have the same positive attitude.

You will probably know exactly what is going on in their lives—you will know how they think and feel about a variety of issues, and you will clearly see what needs changing at your church if the next generation is going to be reached for Christ.

b) Limitations of this stage

You might not be able to lead your group very far, because your life experiences will be not much more developed than theirs. You might need the counsel of some older people to make sure your decisions are wise. You probably won't have a deep biblical perspective on what you do, and you may need others to pull you into line sometimes. In fact, you might find it hard to take correction—I mean, what would those old guys know anyway?

Like being a learner driver, you will probably make a lot of mistakes—and you may cause some accidents along the way! You might try a lot of ideas without really knowing whether they will produce lasting fruit.

While teenagers will readily accept your friendship, they might be reluctant to accept your discipline. Controlling difficult students is often tricky at this stage. Your friendship with them often matters so much to you that you will be reluctant to pull them into line.

You might find it hard to plan long-term, and you might be impatient for everything to be achieved **now**! You may find it hard to cope if your ministry projects don't turn out the way you'd hoped. And you might well feel very discouraged when you see that your group members don't give back to you anywhere near the same amount as what you give out to them.

Although parents may appreciate your getting alongside their teenager, it is unlikely that they will want to accept much ministry from you, or look to you for advice in how to parent successfully!

Stage 2: The "big brother or sister" stage

This is where you're about five to ten years older than the students. Too old to be "one of their friends", but about the right age to be a "big brother" or "big sister". Perhaps your students are aged 15—and you're about 20 to 25. Close in age, but just a little removed.

a) Advantages of this stage
The teenagers will now look up to you more than in the previous stage, and you knowingly or unknowingly will

start to be a role model. You will still be close enough to the kids' culture to understand it well, but you may listen to a different radio station and be a little less in touch with the current fad. You will probably have more money and more access to transport than the students, and so they will start to depend on you more.

You are starting to have a greater understanding of life, and you can give more direction to your students' growth. You have a better idea of what really will work—and what won't work—in ministering to teenagers. You have a little more wisdom, which your group will start to respect. While they still readily accept you as a friend, they are probably more ready to accept discipline from you than when you were in Stage 1.

You've had more time to grow in your own biblical understanding, so your Bible teaching will start to take on greater depth. You will have heard some of their questions many times before, and you will probably have thought though some more helpful answers.

b) Limitations of this stage

You are still ministering to kids from within their own culture, but you might find you are a little more annoyed by them than in Stage 1. Their jokes might start to irritate you. In Stage 1 you might have been quite happy to laugh along at their vulgar bodily functions *(indeed—you may have been the ringleader!)*, but somewhere in Stage 2 you might grow a little tired of it. Parents may start to look at you a bit suspiciously *("Why is that 25-year-old hanging out with my 14-year-old son?")*, and may be reticent to trust their teenagers to you. But once you have won their trust, they will value you as a role model.

You might start to feel "old". It will occur to you that you have had numerous life experiences before some of your group were even born. They won't remember the same things that you do *(after all, they're too young!)*, and they may start to think you're a little old-fashioned on a couple of issues. When you are standing at the back of the hall when some young band is thumping out the latest in modern music, you might suddenly realise: *"I think I'm one of the oldest people in this building!"* You might just work out you don't really **like** their music—in fact, you're not sure that you still belong with these "young kids" any more.

Stage 3: The "uncle or aunty" stage

You are now in your mid-twenties to mid-thirties. This is the first of the longer stages (that is, it lasts for ten or more years). You are now too old to be a "big brother or sister" and too young to be the same age as the kids' mum and dad. So you now take the role of a kindly uncle or aunt.

a) The danger of this stage

This is a dangerous stage. So many youth leaders "drop out" when they hit this stage—because this is the first stage when you start ministering to kids from outside their culture.

Here is what I mean. In the "uncle or aunty" stage, you no longer listen to the same music as the teens. In fact, you probably don't even know the name of most of their songs. And their music is nowhere near as good as the music **you** had in **your** teens! You now watch different movies, wear different clothes, have different mannerisms and go to different places. Your own family situation is often changing, either by simply moving out of home, or perhaps by marrying. You may well have your own young children, and your priorities with your time are changing. If you are not married, you still might be asking deep questions about yourself and what your future holds.

Because you are now no longer a part of youth culture, many youth leaders feel at this stage that they have "lost it". You no longer understand kids, and you feel locked out of their culture.

b) The "difference" of this stage

Many of these differences are true! **But that doesn't mean you have to give up!** It simply means that youth ministry for you is now a **cross-cultural** ministry. That is, you can now reach and penetrate a culture as someone who belongs to another culture. You now live on the planet "adult-land" You are only a visitor to the planet "youth-land". Whether you are a **welcome** visitor depends on how well you acclimatise to doing cross-cultural work.

If you can make this transition, you are set for a long and fruitful youth ministry. I haven't been anywhere **near** youth culture for many a long year. I don't know the intimate details of youth culture—I don't know what their music is—I certainly don't particularly like their music. (Give me classic rock any day!) I am a stranger from another planet. But I am accepted as a visitor into today's youth culture.

c) The advantage of this stage

But here's the good news. To do cross-cultural ministry, you don't have to **join** the culture you are ministering to. You don't have to **pretend** to belong. You don't have to like it or understand it. **You just simply need to understand that their culture exists, and that your teenagers live in it.**

Teenagers will accept any adult—no matter what planet you come from—if you are prepared to give them time. Time. That's all they want. And when you show that you are prepared to spend time—that most valuable of commodities—with them, it speaks powerfully about who you are and what you represent.

Don't pretend you belong to their culture, but simply accept that they are locked in their culture and see everything in terms of their culture. You need to know a little about their culture—and the best way to do this is simply to listen. Hang out with a bunch of teenagers and listen for about half an hour, and you will know enough about their culture to know where the entry points for ministry are.

In Stage 3 your wisdom is growing—your biblical understanding is growing—you are less likely to make the mistakes of Stage 1 and 2. If you have young children, you will often find that teenagers are **fascinated** by young kids, and they will "goo-goo" and "gah-gah" with them all day. You will have a ready supply of baby-sitters, and you may find that students will feel very relaxed about calling around to see you at home. Young people from non-Christian homes may be fascinated to see the way you relate to your own children as a Christian couple. Here is a great opportunity to model to teenagers from non-Christian homes, what a Christian family should look like.

Your students' parents will probably accept you much more, and you may even find you have a ministry with them because of your relationship with their kids. You can also be a great encouragement to younger leaders. You will need to have them around—for their enthusiasm and their ability (as single people) to put in the long hours, without being weighed down by family responsibilities. Because of your experience, you are now in an ideal situation to start training younger leaders.

This is a fantastic stage of youth ministry. Accept that it is now cross-cultural. Don't quit because it is so different, but enjoy it!

Youth ministry gets **easier** every year I get older!

Stage 4: The "parent" stage

This lasts from your mid-thirties to your mid-fifties (or even to your sixties). Quite frankly, you are now close in age to that of the teenagers' own parents. (I have been entrenched in this stage for years!) You may well have teenagers of your own, which will bring you a whole new perspective of how youth ministry looks from a parent's viewpoint!

a) Advantages of this stage

If you managed to make the cultural adjustment in the "uncle or aunty" stage, then the "parents" stage is a breeze! I love it! I am now absolutely from another planet from my teenagers. I get balder and balder and I have a crook back with sciatica. All the kids know I am somehow locked in a time warp from the sixties, but this has got to be the best stage from which to minister to young people. (I haven't got to Stage 5 yet!)

In Stage 4 you can minister with wisdom. I find far more teenagers will come and cry with me now than when I was a younger youth pastor. They will now ask really deep questions about their life, and be accepting of my answers. Their parents too will also turn to oldies like me for wisdom about bringing up their kids. Younger youth leaders look for wisdom as they tread the path that I trod over twenty years ago.

It's taken me this long to actually figure out where I am going in youth ministry. When I look back at my days when I was in my mid twenties, I'm amazed God stuck with me. I had all the enthusiasm in the world, but I had no idea of what I was doing! I would never want to go back there! I long to see the day where we have **stacks and stacks** of youth leaders from the "parent" age.

It's interesting that in smaller churches, with smaller youth groups, it's more common to find parents as youth leaders. They do it "because there's no one else" but it is entirely possible that **they are absolutely the BEST people to be youth leaders**! I always worry about a youth ministry that is entirely led by leaders in their teens and twenties!

b) Limitations of this stage
You need to have lots of Stage 1 and Stage 2 leaders around you. You need someone who can run as fast as your young people. You need someone who can jump off the high rock into the water with them. You need someone who can lunge into a full body tackle in a game of soccer.

I always depend on my Stage 1 and Stage 2 leaders to tell me enough about youth culture so that I can penetrate it. I ask them what a current song is that the kids would know—I ask them who a current sporting hero might be. I ask them what kids are watching on TV, and what makes them laugh. Those Stage 1 and Stage 2 leaders are my eyes and ears. They also tell me when I'm suggesting something which is really old-fashioned and uncool!

The other limitation of this stage is that it is sometimes harder to make initial contact with unchurched teenagers. They will not automatically warm to you like they did when you were younger. But apart from this initial hesitancy, I find that in time, I can develop relationships which are much deeper than I ever had with kids when I was younger.

Can I plead with you—hang on until at least Stage 4 of youth ministry and you will reap so many rewards! (So will the teenagers! So will the kingdom!)

Stage 5: The "grandparent" stage

I haven't got to this one yet, so all this is prophetic. This stage lasts from about late fifties or sixties (certainly from "retirement age") until death. You are now much older than the teenagers' parents—and you fit better into the "grandparent" mould.

I'll write more about this stage when I get there, but I suspect there is a **huge** affinity between teenagers and grandparent figures. Someone once remarked to me that grandchildren and grandparents get on so well because they have a common enemy! I suspect it is more because of the essential difference between parents and grandparents— grandparents have **time**. Oodles of it. And **every** teenager loves that!

Roll on them advancin' years!

Here's what really matters…

You need to understand how your relationship with teenagers will change as you go through these various stages. You need to understand the advantages and the limitations of each stage. But most importantly, **you need to understand the crossover point where you move from ministering to youth from INSIDE their culture, to the point where you minister to them from OUTSIDE their culture**. If you can understand when this transition is happening, determine you won't just bale out because it's getting a little harder, and hang in there long term with your teenagers, then you will have a fantastic and rewarding ministry—and your students will love you for it!

Will you stay in youth ministry long enough to get it right?

Will you become a biblical shepherd and grow a servant heart?

Will you develop your character—so that you become more and more like Jesus?

Will you be committed to changing this upcoming generation so that this world can be won for Christ?

Will you become a "leader who will last"?

Appendices

Appendix 1: Qualities of a Christian leader from four key biblical lists

	1 Timothy 3:1-7	1 Timothy 3:8-13	2 Timothy 3:22-26	Titus 1:5-9	
The one main skill	Able to teach.		Able to teach gently. Instruct those who oppose.	Encourage others by sound doctrine. Refute those who oppose it.	
The one main characteristic	Above reproach.	Sincere.		Blameless, upright, holy, disciplined.	
Eight checkpoints: 1. Check your growth	Not be a recent convert.	Keep hold hof the deep truths of the faith.	Flee the evil desires of youth, pursue righteousness, faith, love and peace.	Hold firmly to the trustworthy message that has been taught.	
2. Check your family relationships	Husband of but one wife. Manage his own family well. Children characterised by obedience and respect.	Husband of but one wife. Manage his household well. Wife characterised by respect and trustworthiness.		Husband of but one wife with children characterised by belief and obedience.	
3. Check your reputation	Respectable. Good reputation with outsiders.	Worthy of respect.			

4. Check your drinking	Habits not given to drunkenness.	Not indulging in much wine.		Not given to drunkenness.
5. Check your temper	Temperate, self-controlled. Not violent, but gentle.			Not overbearing, not quick tempered, not violent, self-controlled.
6. Check your words	Not quarrelsome.		Don't have anything to do with stupid arguments. The Lord's servant must not quarrel.	
7. Check your wallet	Not a lover of money.	Not pursuing dishonest gain.		Not pursuing dishonest gain.
8. Check your attitude	Hospitable.		Kind to everyone. Not resentful.	Loves what is good.

Appendix 2: "Above Reproach"

Setting a biblical example in youth leadership

This is the document that we have put together to help our youth leaders stay "above reproach". It is not meant to be a list of rules—but to give practical guidelines to our leaders to protect not only our young people, but also the reputation of our leaders, and the good name of our youth ministry.

It is important to understand that we uphold the values of this document in the context of God's grace and forgiveness. We don't want to be a community of rules and regulations!

You should also note that this document is updated each year as new issues come to light. You can check our latest version by contacting us at the e-mail address on page ii.

We want a ministry that is characterised by grace and forgiveness—not by rules and regulations. But the Bible is concerned that leaders have a particularly high standard in their personal life. We are to be examples to those whom we lead. By agreeing to become youth leaders at our church we are agreeing to the following standards—which centre on personal growth and integrity.

1. Setting an example—in what we say and what we do (Ephesians 4:29, 5:4)

a) We need to watch carefully our language and our humour to ensure it does not degrade our Lord, or anything good he has created.

b) We will strive to be genuine encouragers who sow positive "words of life" into each other, and into the young people we minister to.

c) We need to be careful that nothing we do or say as leaders could be interpreted as "flirting"—either by our peers, or by group members.

d) The way we dress and present ourselves—while consistent with the culture we are trying to impact—should not be provocative or immodest. We need to be aware of what slogans our T-shirts display, and what more subtle messages our appearance sends out. Leaders need to be particularly aware of this at swimming activities. What we do should never be the opportunity for someone else to stumble.

2. Setting an example—in our use of alcohol/smoking (1 Tim 3:8, 1 Corinthians 8:13)

a) While personal use of alcohol / smoking is a private decision, all youth leaders are strongly encouraged to consider abstaining for the sake of their ministries.

b) Drunkenness is specifically shown to be disobedient in the Bible (Ephesians 5:18). We must ensure that this sin does not characterise our lifestyle! So, while youth leaders may well be involved with non-Christian adult friends who both drink and get drunk, leaders should not be encouraging this at their own functions. Certainly, leaders should not be invite group members to functions where there is the likelihood of guests getting drunk.

c) Because of the high profile of alcohol / smoking in our society, and the easy misinterpretation by a young person of any "approval" of this in the lifestyle of their leader, no youth leader should normally be consuming alcohol or smoking where there are students present.

d) Alcohol / smoking should not be present at any youth group activity. No leader should have been consuming alcohol or smoking before interacting with young people.

3. Setting an example—in our personal relationships (Ephesians 5:3, 1 Timothy 3:2)

a) Our relationships with the opposite sex are to be "above reproach". We must not place ourselves in situations where our integrity might be seen to be compromised. No youth leader should be "spending the night" unsupervised in the same proximity as a member of the opposite sex (eg:—two alone in a house/tent overnight etc). We need to be careful about the "uninterruptable aloneness" that we spend with our boy/girlfriend.

b) No youth leader should be romantically linked with any high school student. The only exception is where there is a pre-existing student/student relationship (eg: a Yr 12 & Yr 11 are dating, and the following year the ex-Yr 12 becomes a leader. The ex-Yr 12 can still lead, but not in the age group where their partner is.)

c) No youth leader should be romantically linked with a non-Christian.

4. Setting an example—in our relationships with young people

a) Our relationships with younger people are extremely privileged. No abuse of this relationship is tolerated. There is an official protocol in place for dealing with any abuse of young people by church workers. This involves calling the police. There will be no "protection" for those who abuse our young people.

b) Male students are to be counselled only by male leaders, and female students are to be counselled only by female leaders. If a student of the opposite sex requests personal counselling from you, involve a leader of the opposite sex straight away. All three of you can then continue talking.

c) You should never be alone with any student in a non-public place. If you need to talk privately (eg: counselling, pastoral work, individual discipling etc), then do it where you can be easily interrupted. (Eg: In a house, where there are other people in other rooms; at the side of the hall, when there are other people passing; in an open park, where you are clearly visible for a long distance, in an office with a glass door, etc)

d) You should not visit an individual student in their home, unless there are others present. You should not have an individual student in your home unless there are others present.

e) You should never be alone with an individual group member overnight in the same house/tent etc. Always work in groups larger than just the two of you.

f) When you are the only person in your car, you should never give a lift to an individual student of the opposite sex. If you are transporting a group, the last person you drop off must be a member of the same sex—even if this means going out of your way. The alternative is to have another adult with you.

g) Physical contact with young people is a vital part of affirming and strengthening relationships. Please use it! (Handshakes, pat on the shoulder etc) But we need to be careful that our physical touching will not be misinterpreted. Do not hug students of the opposite sex!

h) Leaders need to make sure that their contact with young people of the opposite sex is not open to misinterpretation. No leader should be regularly phoning, writing to, or visiting a student of the opposite sex. Where needed, this sort of contact must be only occasional, in accordance with the above guidelines. Similarly, while a leader might have occasional or brief contact with a young person of the opposite sex via the internet (E-mail, ICQ etc) or SMS, no leader should have, lengthy, frequent or "deep" discussion with students of the opposite sex via their computer or phone.

i) To maintain our position of integrity, no leader should partner a high-school student of the opposite sex to any social function—including end-of-year School Formals.

6. Setting an example—in our submission
a) We will model submission to those who have pastoral oversight over us (Hebrews 13: 17).

b) Our obedience to the governing authorities (eg: road rules, copyright etc) should be evidenced by our lifestyle (Romans 13:1).

c) We will submit to one another out of reverence for Christ (Ephesians 5:21). When we fail to maintain biblical standards, we need to understand and model the God who is full of grace and forgiveness. We need to know that where we ourselves have failed God by our continuing sin, that we have a God who wants us back, who calls us to repentance, and is ready to offer forgiveness (Ephesians 4:32).

d) For any breach of these guidelines—do not panic! It is not the end of the world! We still love you dearly! But if there is any breach—accidentally or intentionally—the

Appendix 3: Bible-teaching resources

This reading list is provided to help youth leaders to read, understand, and teach the Bible better.

1. Helpful guides on "How" to read the Bible (the principles of interpretation)

Gordon D. Fee & Douglas Stuart, *How to Read the Bible for All Its Worth*, 2nd edn. (Grand Rapids: Zondervan 1993)— aims to introduce the reader to all the various types of literature found within the Bible, and to provide tips on how to interpret and apply each type. This is simply the best introductory book on Bible interpretation around.

Postcard from Palestine, 2nd edn. (Kingsford: St Matthias Press 1997)—has similar aims to *How to Read the Bible for All Its Worth*, but written at a simpler level.

2. Helpful guides to the content of the Bible

Gordon D. Fee & Douglas Stuart, *How to Read the Bible Book by Book* (Grand Rapids: Zondervan 2002)—the companion volume to *How to Read the Bible for All Its Worth*. Takes the reader through each biblical book, summarising its contents, and providing a specific guide to interpretation.

Mark Strom, *The Symphony of Scripture* (Phillipsburg: Presbyterian and Reformed 2001)—Strom analyses the way each individual book of the Bible contributes to the unified message of salvation found within the Scriptures. Invaluable help for putting the two Testaments of the Bible together.

3. Useful reference works

Pat Alexander & David Alexander (eds.), *New Lion Handbook to the Bible*, 3rd edn. (Oxford: Lion 1999)—beautifully illustrated, this large reference work provides an outline of the message of each biblical book, as well as conveying crucial background information.

I.H. Marshall, et.al., *New Bible Dictionary*, 3rd edn. (Leicester: Intervarsity Press 1996)—if you have ever wondered where Jabesh-Gilead is, or wanted to explain the term 'sanctification', this book will tell you the answers, and so much more! It is no overstatement to say that every significant word or concept in the Bible is discussed in this volume. The best money you may ever spend.

Other titles by Tim Hawkins:

- **Fruit that will last**
- **Disciples who will last**
- **Discovering Jesus Bible studies**
- **Discipleship Training Series**

Most of these titles are available from The Good Book Company:

In the UK: www.thegoodbook.co.uk
tel: 0845 225 0880; admin@thegoodbook.co.uk

In N America: www.thegoodbook.com
admin@thegoodbook.com

In New Zealand: www.thegoodbook.co.nz
admin@thegoodbook.co.nz

In Australia:
Hawkins Ministry Resources www.hawkinsministry.com
info@hawkinsministry.com

This is Tim's own site where all his material is available. As well as all his books and Bible studies, you can find DVDs and CDs with great teaching material for both leaders and students.

There is an array of youth ministry resources here—much of which is not found on any other website.
